LANDING YOUR DREAM JOB

Step-by-Step Guide

CHRISTINE FREY

NEXT CHAPTER
Press

Landing on Your Dream Job

© 2024 Christine Frey

Published by Next Chapter Press

All rights reserved. No part of this book may be reproduced, distributed, or transmitted in any form or by any means, including photocopying, recording, or other electronic or mechanical methods, without the prior written permission of the publisher, except in the case of brief quotations embodied in reviews and certain other non-commercial uses permitted by copyright law.

For permissions inquiries, contact:

Next Chapter Press

[ktkchristine@gmail.com]

ISBN No. 9781068330315

First Edition: December 2024

This is a work of nonfiction. While every effort has been made to ensure accuracy, the author and publisher make no representations or warranties concerning the accuracy or completeness of the contents.

To

Everyone chasing their dreams!

Synopsis

Packed with insider secrets and actionable tips, this book is your ultimate job-hunting toolkit—whether you're a recent grad, career changer, or seasoned professional looking for a fresh start.

After reading this book, you'll be armed with everything you need to:

- Craft a CV so irresistible that employers will be lining up to meet you.
- Uncover job search hacks most people don't even know exist.
- Walk into any interview with total confidence and own the room.
- Know exactly how to answer the trickiest interview questions.
- Ask thoughtful, memorable questions that leave a lasting impression.
- Research companies like an insider and dazzle them with your knowledge.
- Highlight your skills and experience to stand out as the perfect fit.
- Dress to impress and make a stellar first impression.
- Follow up smartly and stay top-of-mind with hiring managers.

With proven strategies to make a lasting impression and secure the role of your dreams, this book is your key to success.

Table of Content

Chapter 1: Prepping for the Job Hunt – Time to Get Real! 1

Chapter 2: Crafting Your CV: Stand Out and Get Noticed! 12

Chapter 3: Why Bother with a Cover Letter? Here's Why! 33

Chapter 4: Beyond the Basics: Innovative Places to Start Your Job Search 43

Chapter 5: Research the Company – The Key to Interview Success! 62

Chapter 6: Prepared for the Questions (and How Not to Sound Like a Robot!) 70

Chapter 7: Smart Questions to Ask—And the Ones You Should Skip 83

Chapter 8: Dressed to Kill or to Be Killed? 89

Chapter 9: The Big Interview Day – Mastering the Countdown ... 96

Chapter 10: Post-interview – Time to Relax (But Don't Get Too Cozy!) 106

Chapter 1
Prepping for the Job Hunt – Time to Get Real!

Most people think landing a dream job means throwing on some kind of mask—pretending to be someone they're not, saying what they think recruiters want to hear. But plot twist! The truth is, finding your dream job is more like finding yourself. No, seriously. Think of it as a scavenger hunt where the clues are hidden in your personality, strengths, and quirks. And by the end, you might actually like the person you've uncovered along the way. Who knew, right?

Landing a job that doesn't align with who you truly are isn't just a minor inconvenience; it's a recipe for burnout. I've seen it happen too many times: people stuck in roles that clash with their values, strengths, or personality. And guess what? It's not pretty. They're constantly stressed, drained, and eventually, they feel trapped. No one should have to drag themselves to work every day, dreading each hour. Trust me, if you settle for a job that doesn't resonate with you, it'll feel like trying to fit a square peg into a round hole—frustrating and exhausting in the long run. So, let's avoid that pitfall, shall we?

Listen, I know you might be sitting there thinking, "But what if I'm just not dream job material?" Maybe you're worried you don't have enough experience, or maybe you're fixating on those little weaknesses that seem bigger than they really are. Here's the truth: every single person—yes, even you—has strengths, skills, and qualities that make them valuable. You're not some blank slate with nothing to offer; you've got stories, experiences, talents, and even quirks that can light up the right room or fit the perfect role.

Think about it: there are thousands of jobs out there, each with unique needs. Somewhere, there's one waiting for exactly what you bring to the table. Maybe it's your knack for problem-solving, your creative spark, your ability to connect with others, or even that weird talent for organizing chaos. Employers don't just hire perfect people (spoiler alert: they don't exist). They hire real people who bring something special to the mix—people just like you.

So stop comparing yourself to some ideal version of a "perfect candidate" that probably doesn't exist. Instead, focus on finding the job that sees the real you as the perfect fit. Because trust me, there's one out there. And when you find it, you'll realize your strengths—and even your so-called weaknesses—were exactly what was needed all along.

But here's the thing: personal charm can be just as important as your experience and qualifications. When you walk into an interview, it's not just about what you say—it's about the energy you bring. Recruiters can sense if you're enthusiastic, confident, and genuinely excited about the opportunity. And yes, that charm is just as critical as it is on a first date! Your vibe speaks volumes before you've even said a word, and it can be the difference between a memorable impression and a forgettable one.

So, prepare to show the most authentic, enthusiastic version of yourself. It's not about being perfect; it's about being real. Smile, engage, and let your passion shine through. Believe me, recruiters don't just see it—they feel it. And that kind of energy? It's magnetic. The right job is as much about the connection you create as the skills you bring. Make it count.

Now that you've got your mindset dialed in, it's time to roll up your sleeves and do a bit of homework. (Yeah, sorry—not even adulthood lets you escape cramming.) So, grab your favorite cup of coffee, put on that one power anthem that makes you feel like you own the world, and get ready for some serious soul-searching.

Ask yourself the big questions: What do you really want to do? What makes you actually excited to get out of bed? No, I'm not talking about what looks cool on LinkedIn or what sounds impressive at family reunions. I mean the thing that makes you feel alive on a random Tuesday morning. The kind of work that feels meaningful, exciting, and authentically you.

Then, think about what you should be doing. What's going to keep you motivated and engaged day after day? And most importantly—what are you really, truly great at? You know, the thing you're so good at that people come to you for help with it, or you completely lose track of time when you're doing it. Those are your secret weapons, my friend. When you can bring them all together, that's when the magic happens.

This phase is all about tuning in to your internal GPS. Most people skip it because they're eager to hit "apply" like a contestant on a game show slamming the buzzer. But trust me, this reflection time will save you from that awful "How did I end up here?" feeling later. Think of it as creating a roadmap for your career—once you've got that, everything else falls into place.

Back in the day, I was a Business Development Manager at a reputable company, leading a team of seven supervisors and 30 sales. Most of them were fantastic, but one supervisor—let's call him Bob—was the outlier. Bob wasn't exactly the poster child for enthusiasm. He was always late, his colleagues were endlessly grumbling about him, and the team vibe was, well, less *team* and more *meh*.

I decided to have a heart-to-heart with Bob. Turns out, he wasn't lazy—he was just in the wrong job. Bob was an introvert, and dealing with clients and team dynamics drained him faster than my phone battery on a road trip. But when we talked about data? Oh, the man lit up like a slot machine jackpot! Bob didn't just love numbers; he was obsessed with finding patterns in piles of data.

Cue the lightbulb moment: I recommended Bob transfer to the IS (Information Services) Department. It was a perfect match. Bob thrived in his new role, diving headfirst into data analysis and uncovering trends that helped us shape razor-sharp sales strategies. Thanks to his insights, we started making decisions that actually made sense—imagine that!

Bob went from being "that guy everyone complains about" to "the genius who makes us look good." He felt fulfilled, gained massive respect from his colleagues, and became an invaluable asset to the company.

What I learned? Sometimes people aren't failing—they're just in the wrong seat on the bus. Helping someone find their sweet spot can transform not just their career, but the entire team's success. And hey, the world needs more pattern-finders like Bob.

When I was a Sales Director for a media company, I had my hands full managing sales targets for magazine advertising and event management. While the magazine side was cruising along nicely, the event sales? Not so much—it was lagging like a snail in a marathon.

One day, an administrative staff member approached me, eager to chat about her dreams. Let's call her Sarah. Sarah had been with the company for five years, stuck in a role that clearly wasn't lighting her fire. She told me she had talked to not one but *two* previous Sales Directors about her aspiration to move into event sales, but nothing had ever come of it. She was articulate, determined, and honestly, I could tell she was itching for a chance to shine.

So, I thought, "Why not see what she's made of?" I invited Sarah to accompany me on a visit to one of our advertisers to pitch an event. Sarah came armed with preparation, and when it was her turn to speak, she completely nailed it. She asked insightful questions, zeroed in on the advertiser's needs, and presented ideas so smoothly that I almost wanted to buy the event myself! Watching her in action, delivering a masterclass in consultative selling, was a delight.

Right then and there, I knew she belonged on the event sales team. I officially placed her in the role, and, as they say, the rest was history. Not only did she exceed expectations, but her energy and fresh perspective also revitalized the team and helped us crush our event sales targets.

These stories taught me an invaluable lesson: sometimes, incredible talent is right under your nose, just waiting to be noticed—first by you, and then by your employer! They also serve as a powerful reminder that a fulfilling job doesn't just elevate a career—it can completely transform a person's confidence, happiness, and sense of purpose.

Alright, now you understand how crucial it is to uncover your talents—but how do you actually identify your strengths and weaknesses? Here are a few ways to get started:

- **Stare Into Your Soul (aka Self-Reflection)**
  Grab a cup of coffee (or tea if you're fancy) and think about your life. When did you feel like a rock star? And when did you want to crawl under a rock? Your strengths are the things you can do on autopilot, and your weaknesses are the things you dread doing—like assembling IKEA furniture.

- **Take Those Weird Personality Tests**
  You know those quizzes that tell you if you're more of a Golden Retriever or a Slytherin? Yeah, but this time with grown-up names like **Myers-Briggs**, **StrengthsFinder**, or **DISC**. These tests are designed to gently break it to you that maybe you're not as organized as you thought, but hey, at least you're super creative!

- **Ask Your Friends (But Bribe Them First)**
  Who better to tell you how awesome or *questionable* you are than the people who see you mess up regularly? Gather feedback from friends, family, co-workers—anyone who's seen you in action. But be prepared; you might hear things like, "You're great at showing up late to meetings." Ah, honesty.

- **Check Your Report Card (aka Performance Reviews)**
Remember that time your boss gave you a "suggestion" to improve? That's code for "weakness alert." And when they praised you for saving the project last minute? Bingo—that's a strength. Performance reviews are like school report cards, except no one hangs them on the fridge.

- **Go Do Something You're Terrible At**
Want to really get to know yourself? Try something new, something you're pretty sure you'll stink at—like salsa dancing or assembling that IKEA bookshelf we talked about. You'll quickly figure out what comes naturally (probably not the dancing) and what makes you break out in a cold sweat.

- **SWOT It Out**
Do a little DIY **SWOT analysis**: Strengths, Weaknesses, Opportunities, and Threats. It's like the pros-and-cons list but with fancier words. Your strengths and weaknesses are all about you; the opportunities and threats are how the world is messing with you—like the opportunity to impress your boss by meeting that deadline and the threat of Netflix releasing a new season of your favorite show.

- **Hire a Professional (Because Sometimes You Just Need a Third Party)**
Consider getting a coach—no, not the kind that yells at you to do push-ups, but a **career or life coach**. They can help you figure out what makes you shine and what makes you hide under your desk, all with a positive, "You've got this!" attitude.

Afterwards, we'll break this down step by step to help you figure out your strengths and interests. Yeah, I know—it might sound like something straight out of a middle school guidance counselor's playbook. But seriously, if you asked 100 people on the street what they're genuinely good at, maybe five of them could give you a clear answer. Be part of that five percent!

Once you've nailed down your strengths and interests, you can use this knowledge to identify which jobs are the best fit for you.

1. Introvert or Extrovert: Pick Your Lane

First things first—let's talk personality. If the idea of small talk at a networking event makes you want to curl up in a ball, congrats! You're likely an introvert. That's a big hint that jobs in sales or customer service might not be your jam. Instead, consider roles where you can work behind the scenes, like data analysis, graphic design, or even warehouse work. Seriously, embrace the peace and quiet.

Now, if you're more of the "chats up strangers in the coffee line" type, you're probably an extrovert, and sitting in a cubicle all day doing repetitive tasks would probably drive you bananas. For you, social interaction is key—so roles that involve working with people, like marketing, team leadership, or, yes, sales, might be where you'll shine.

No matter where you fall on the spectrum, knowing your personality type is crucial. It helps you figure out the kind of work environment where you'll thrive, not just survive. Trust me, there's a big difference. Once you've figured out if you're a social butterfly or a lone wolf, it's time to decide whether you're drawn to technical or non-technical roles.

2. Technical or Non-Technical: Where Do You Belong?

Are you one of those people who lights up when they get to geek out over tech specs and algorithms? If so, a technical role might be your ticket. Maybe you love writing code, analyzing data, or fixing tech problems for your friends and family (whether you want to or not). Careers like software development, IT support, or data analysis could be a perfect fit.

But if all that sounds like a foreign language and you're more interested in big ideas, communication, and creativity, non-technical roles are calling your name. These are jobs where you can flex those people skills, strategic thinking, and problem-solving abilities—like marketing, project management, or even customer relations.

And don't worry if you feel torn between the two. Hybrid roles exist, and plenty of jobs blend technical know-how with creative problem-solving. The key is to play to your strengths.

3. Aesthetics and Strategy: Where's Your Happy Place?

If you've got a keen eye for visuals and a natural flair for design, you're probably drawn to aesthetic-focused roles. Careers like graphic design, interior decorating, or makeup artistry might be perfect for you. You'll get to create, make things beautiful, and put your artistic talents to good use.

But if you're more of a puzzle solver—someone who thrives on crafting the perfect plan or figuring out complex problems— you're a strategist at heart. Roles like project management or management consulting are right up your alley. You'll love navigating through challenges and turning chaos into order, all while impressing everyone with your master plans.

4. Onsite or Remote

Ah, the big question: Where will you work? Not long ago, the answer was simple—you went to an office, sat in a cubicle, and pretended not to notice the endless supply of donuts in the break room (pro tip: *always* take a donut). Now, thanks to the rise of remote and hybrid work, you've got options. Let's break it down.

- Office life: If you enjoy structure, routine, and a wardrobe that consists of more than sweatpants, then office life might be your jam. You get to see people face-to-face (no lagging Zoom calls!), collaborate in real time, and even go out for after-work drinks (see extroverts, above). The downside? You're probably going to be stuck in traffic, and let's face it, parking never gets any easier.

- Remote work: Want to work in your pajamas and commute from your bed to your kitchen? Remote work is calling your name. Remote jobs offer flexibility, and you get to skip the office drama (and those meetings that should have been emails). But before you go fully remote, know that it's not all rainbows and kittens from here on out. It can get lonely, and you might miss the camaraderie of in-person work. Plus, you'll need to resist the urge to "just take a quick nap" or "the siren calls of Netflix" — trust me, it never ends well.

- <u>Hybrid model</u>: The best of both worlds, right? In a hybrid role, you'll spend some days in the office and others working from home. It's perfect for people who want flexibility but still crave occasional in-person interaction and a bit structure. Just be prepared for a slightly chaotic schedule and the constant need to figure out what day it is.

Chapter 2
Crafting Your CV: Stand Out and Get Noticed!

Alright, let's cut to the chase. You've got dreams, ambition, and probably a favorite snack to munch on while browsing through job listings. But before you hit "Apply Now" on your dream gig, there's one crucial thing you need—a knockout CV. Think of it as your personal hype sheet. It's like the résumé equivalent of a first date, and you want to make a great impression—without all the awkward small talk.

So, how do you write a CV that makes hiring managers pause, instead of tossing it into the rejection pile faster than you can say "Dear Sir/Madam"? Let's break it down.

1. CV Tailoring: Because One Size Doesn't Fit All!

Generic CVs are about as appealing as stale popcorn. You need to tailor that baby!

Think about it: having a business degree or engineering experience isn't going to make you stand out. The hiring manager has probably seen 127 other applicants with the exact same credentials. They're all qualified, and they all look great on paper. So why should they hire you?

Here's the secret sauce: don't just tell them you have a degree or experience—everybody's got that. Instead, grab that job description like it's your roadmap to the final interview. Study it, highlight it, sleep with it under your pillow if you have to. Then, connect the dots between what they want and what you bring.

Have a knack for solving problems under pressure? Talk about the time you streamlined a process at work and saved the day (bonus points if you were wearing a metaphorical superhero cape). Aspiring to lead a team someday? Show how your personality and goals fit the company culture and its big-picture dreams.

If the job is all about "team leadership" and "project management," don't just slap down that time you coordinated the office pizza party. Highlight how you led a team to conquer a massive project like a boss. Maybe you spearheaded a campaign that increased brand engagement by 50%, or managed a social media blitz that got people talking (and not just your mom).

It's not just about saying, "I fit the role." It's about making the hiring manager think, "Wow, this person was made for this role." When you align your education, experience, personality, and ambition with what they're asking for, you're not just another applicant—you're their most valuable player.

Oh, and sprinkle in a dash of confidence. After all, you're not just applying for the job—you're basically saying, "This role is my destiny." Who wouldn't want to hire someone like that?

And remember, hiring managers today often use AI to screen CVs, so it's crucial to use the same terminology they're looking for. If the job description calls for "B2B consultative sales," don't just mention you have over 10 years of sales experience—specifically show how your experience fits into consultative selling in a B2B context.

If the job is about robotic product design, don't just brag about your endless engineering experience—instead, drop some details about that cool robotic design project you worked on and what you actually accomplished. Did you build a robot that assembles gadgets faster than a coffee-fueled engineer? Awesome. Mention it!

This way, your CV won't just pass the AI screening; it'll also grab the attention of the humans behind it too!

2. Formatting: Keep It Short and Sweet

Think of your CV like your outfit for a job interview—you want it neat, professional, and not overly complicated.

Start with your name and contact details at the top, like you're opening a strong email intro: "Hi, I'm awesome, and here's how to reach me!" Use consistent fonts (no Comic Sans, please) and make sure your job titles don't look like an afterthought squished into the margins. This isn't art class; it's your career!

Keep the CV to one or two pages. This is CV, not a novel! Nobody's got time to read your life story, no matter how riveting it is. If you've been working for over 30 years, resist the urge to include every job you've ever had. No one needs to know about that summer gig flipping burgers in the '80s. Instead, focus on your last two roles, especially the ones that scream, 'I'm perfect for this job!' Leave the rest for your memoir.

If you're a recent graduate with little to no job experience, don't stress—highlight your personal traits – problem-solving, teamwork, time management, attentive to details – give real life examples, for time management, you can say, "Balanced full-time studies with part-time work, mastering prioritization and meeting deadlines efficiently." You can highlight what you learned from extracurricular activities, and explain and the strengths you displayed.

3. A Killer Professional Summary: Hook Them from the Start!

The professional summary is your elevator pitch, and nobody likes a rambling ride—unless you're stuck with a talkative coworker. Be bold, be concise, and sell your story! Here's what to include:

- **Who you are**: Kick things off with a punch. Are you an "Aspiring ninja of digital marketing" or a "Master of all things tech"? Make it catchy!

- **Your expertise**: Drop some key skills like they're hot potatoes. Think "data-driven project wrangler" or "creative content magician"—show them your magic!

- **Relevant experience**: Give a quick nod to your experience—"Five years of saving the day in the sales department" or "Ten years of making brands sparkle." You want them to know you've been around the block!

- **Your value proposition**: What makes you the unicorn in a sea of horses? Maybe you've got a "proven track record of turning frowns into brand loyalty" or "expertise in making numbers dance."

- **Your goal or vision**: Wrap it up with what you're after. How about "Ready to sprinkle my magic on your marketing team" or "Looking to unleash my superpowers in creative strategy"?

- **Personal charm**: Don't forget to sprinkle in a dash of your personality! Maybe you "enjoy the buzz of teamwork and camaraderie" or "known for bringing the fun while getting things done." Your charm can be the cherry on top!

So instead of saying, "I'm a hard worker who enjoys teamwork," you should create a more 3-dimensional image of who you are and make sure that the employer can't wait to meet you. Below are just some examples of professional summary:

1) **The Data Dynamo**
   "Analytical wizard with a knack for turning raw data into game-changing insights. With six years of experience optimizing business strategies, I've saved teams time, money, and plenty of headaches. Passionate about making numbers tell compelling stories and excited to supercharge your analytics team."

2) **The Creative Strategist**
   "Bold content creator and marketing strategist with over a decade of experience crafting campaigns that not only wow audiences but align perfectly with company goals. Known for turning big ideas into even bigger results, I thrive on collaboration and the adrenaline rush of making brands truly unforgettable."

3) **The Tech Trailblazer**
   "Tech-savvy innovator with a proven track record of solving complex problems and building scalable solutions. With 8+ years of experience in software development and

systems architecture, I specialize in creating seamless user experiences."

4) The Sales Whisperer
"Relationship-builder extraordinaire with a flair for closing deals and a decade of sales success. From boosting revenue to creating win-win partnerships, I'm all about delivering value. Known for turning cold calls into warm friendships!"

5) The Operations Pro
"Master of streamlined operations with over 12 years of experience in optimizing workflows and managing high-performing teams. I thrive in fast-paced environments, love turning chaos into efficiency, and am ready to bring my organizational magic to your growing business."

6) The Product Pioneer
"Creative product manager with a love for solving user pain points and driving innovation. Over six years of experience launching successful products that delight customers and exceed revenue goals. Excited to bring my vision and adaptability to your team."

4. Facts Over Fiction: Quantify Your Success

Look, nobody's impressed by vague buzzwords like "improved efficiency" or "boosted performance." What does that even mean? But if you throw in some hard numbers—like "increased sales by 35%" or "saved the company $100K a year"—now we're talking. Numbers are like your personal superhero cape. They swoop in and make your accomplishments look way more impressive than a vague "I did some good stuff."

Hiring managers are busy. They don't have time to guess how amazing you are. When you say you grew sales by 35%, they can picture the impact right away. And if you're still wondering why numbers matter: because anyone can say they "led a successful project," but can they show they led a project that resulted in a $500K deal? Didn't think so.

Basically, quantifying your achievements is like adding a cherry on top of an already fabulous sundae. It's not bragging, it's just the facts, and facts are what seal the deal. So go ahead, drop those digits, and let your achievements do the talking. Cha-ching!

Here are some examples that quantify achievements and impress the employers:

1) **Increased Sales**
   "Boosted sales by 40% in one year by launching a targeted email campaign, leading to a $1.2M increase in revenue. Recognized as the top performer for three consecutive quarters."

2) **Customer Retention**
   "Improved customer retention by 18% within six months through a targeted loyalty program, reducing churn rates and increasing lifetime value by an average of $400 per customer."

3) **Building Partnerships**
   "Developed a strategic partnership with a leading industry player, resulting in a new joint venture that

increased brand visibility and generated $300K in new business opportunities within the first six months."

4) **Team Leadership during Change**
"Led a cross-functional team through a major company restructuring, maintaining morale and exceeding productivity targets by 15% during the transition. Championed regular check-ins and created a transparent communication plan that kept everyone engaged and focused."

5) **Innovation**
"Created a new project management system that reduced project delivery times by 25%, improving team collaboration and saving the company an estimated $80K annually in overtime costs."

6) **Cost Savings**
"Negotiated new vendor contracts that resulted in a 20% reduction in supply costs, saving the company $150K annually without sacrificing quality or service."

7) **Product Launch Success**
"Led the successful launch of a new product line that exceeded projected sales by 60%, contributing an additional $500K in revenue in the first quarter alone."

But what if your wins aren't just about the numbers? Intangible achievements matter too! For example:

1) **Team Leadership**
   "Led a team through a major restructuring, ensuring high morale and continued productivity during a challenging transition. Maintained strong employee engagement while navigating organizational changes."

2) **Process Improvement**
   "Streamlined the customer onboarding process, significantly improving overall client satisfaction. Developed and implemented a new inventory management system, improving efficiency and reducing operational bottlenecks."

3) **Building Partnerships**
   "Cultivated a strategic partnership with a key industry player, opening doors to new business opportunities. Fostered long-term relationships with stakeholders, driving continuous collaboration and increased revenue potential."

4) **Crisis Management**
   "Managed a high-pressure product recall affecting tens of thousands of customers, coordinating cross-functional teams to resolve the issue within 72 hours. Developed a transparent communication strategy that preserved customer trust and minimized reputational damage."

5. Display Your Skills: Season with Your Unique Touch!

Skills make or break your CV, so don't just list them like you're ticking off boxes. Make them sing. If you're a design wizard, don't just say "proficient in Adobe Creative Suite" like it's some boring chore—tell them you can whip up stunning visuals faster than most people can open PowerPoint. Or, if you're a customer service pro, don't just claim you're a good communicator—show how your charm keeps clients happy even when everything's on fire. Paint a picture—unless you're applying for a painting job, then yeah, maybe literally!

And don't forget, the AI is watching! Matching your skills to the job description tremendously increases your chances of being selected for an interview. If they ask for 'stakeholder management,' don't assume 'account management' will slide through. It's like ordering a steakburger and getting a cheeseburger—close, but not what they wanted. The same goes for 'proficiency in HubSpot'—saying 'I know my way around CRMs' won't cut it. Be specific, or the robots (and the hiring managers) won't be impressed!

Bottom line: no more one-size-fits-all CVs. Each job is like a new recipe—unique ingredients, exact skills. Showcase your skills with the right keywords to pass the AI's test and show the humans you're the secret sauce they've been looking for!

6. Experience: Less Could Be More

You've done a lot, I get it. But let's focus on what matters. Your experience must match what they're asking for because hiring managers (and their trusty AI sidekicks) are like detectives, searching for the exact skills they need. If your CV is all over the place, it's like showing up to a pizza party with sushi—cool, but not what anyone ordered.

Remember, hiring managers don't have the time (or patience) to sift through your entire life story. They're looking for the specific experiences that prove you can do the job. If you've built financial models that saved your company millions, shout that from the rooftops! But leave your experience of waiting tables at a Michelin-star restaurant for when you're applying to be a head waiter at a high-end spot. Otherwise, it's just noise.

Employers aren't interested in what you did 30 years ago—they want to know how you can make their lives easier *now*. So don't make them search for the pearl in a stack of hay! When you show relevant experience, it's like saying, "Hey, I've solved this problem before, and I can do it again." But don't just toss in random jobs for the sake of filling space. If you can't connect the dots between what you've done and what they need, they won't either—and they might think you're just padding your CV.

7. Education & Certifications: Only Showcase What Matters

You earned that fancy degree—so flaunt it! Start with your highest qualification, like "MBA from Business School X." No one needs to know about your perfect attendance in kindergarten, but if you've got certifications that give you an edge? Definitely throw those in. Just make sure they're relevant.

If you're applying for a project manager role, highlight your *PMP Certification* and any specific methodologies you've mastered, like *Agile or Scrum*. Leave out that yoga instructor certification—unless you're planning to implement some Zen techniques into your project management style!

For a digital marketing position, supply your Google Analytics Certification or Facebook Blueprint Certification. Don't include that time you took a one-off course on balloon animals; it's not going to help you craft a killer marketing strategy!

When applying for a sales position, emphasize any relevant certifications, such as Certified Sales Professional (CSP) or Salesforce Certification. No one needs to know about your certification in cookie baking—even if your cookies are delicious!

8. Proofread Like a Hawk

Yes, typos happen. But they should not happen on your CV. Mistakes showed your attitude that you did not vale the role that much, it could also show to the hiring manager that you are a sloppy and careless person. Imagine you're the hiring manager juggling 200 applications, and you see "expereinced manager." Next stop: Trash can. Proofread like your job depends on it—because it does. A clean, error-free CV screams "I care about the details," which is something every boss loves to hear

9. Should You Add a Photo? It's a Toss-Up!

Ah, the great CV photo debate—should you include one or not? Well, the jury's still out on this one. Some employers might feel a photo invades privacy or invites bias. If the job listing specifically says no photo, that's your cue to skip it. But if there's no mention of it? Adding a photo could be a game-changer.

Here's the deal: If you're going to include a picture, make it count. Think LinkedIn-level professional—not the candid shot from your cousin's wedding where you're holding a champagne flute.

Choose a photo that shows you looking approachable and polished. Bonus points if you smile! Studies show that smiling in photos exudes confidence and warmth. (It's true—science says so!) Just don't go overboard; this isn't your passport picture, so aim for natural and friendly.

And please, for the love of first impressions, no selfies, no tropical beach backgrounds, and definitely no pics with your dog—even if he's the cutest pup on the planet. Save those gems for Instagram or your holiday cards.

At the end of the day, your CV isn't just a rundown of your achievements—it's your personal highlight reel. Whether you add a photo or not, make sure your CV radiates professionalism, personality, and precision. Show off the best, brightest, most hire-worthy version of yourself. Do that, and you'll have hiring managers eager to hit that "call" button.

10. No Working Experience: Fresh Grads and Newcomers, This One's for You!

So you're stepping into the job market as a fresh grad or a new immigrant. Maybe you don't have a network of local professionals to vouch for you or a track record in this particular industry. Fear not—you can still craft a compelling CV that makes hiring managers stop and take notice. Here's how.

- **Highlight Transferable Skills Like a Seasoned Expert**
  You might not have direct experience, but chances are you've picked up some seriously valuable skills along the way. Did you lead a project during school or at a previous job that required organization, communication, and time

management? Boom—those are transferable skills every employer loves. Did you handle customer service or adapt to a new environment? You're showing resilience and adaptability, which are gold in any workplace.

Maybe you've also worked on a team or collaborated on a group project—showing you're a team player with strong collaboration and problem-solving skills. Employers want people who can work well with others and tackle challenges together!

Example:
"In my previous role as a project coordinator for a university event, I led a small team to manage logistics, delegated tasks, and ensured all deadlines were met. This experience helped me develop strong organizational skills and the ability to communicate clearly under pressure." or "During my internship in customer service, I adapted quickly to handling diverse customer inquiries, which strengthened my problem-solving and conflict resolution skills—valuable assets in any fast-paced work environment."

- **Make Your Education and Training Work Hard for You**

    For fresh graduates, list out relevant courses, projects, and any standout grades. Mention skills gained through internships or group projects that tie into the job description. For immigrants, don't forget to showcase any retraining, certifications, or local qualifications you've earned to help bridge gaps in local industry norms.

    Even if the experience doesn't sound immediately relevant, draw out skills that are. For example, if you have a degree in economics but are applying for a marketing role, mention how you analyzed data or conducted research—these skills translate well!

Example:
"As a graduate with a degree in Economics, I developed strong analytical skills through courses in data analysis and market research, which are highly applicable to my current interest in a marketing role." or "With a degree in Computer Science, I gained a strong foundation in problem-solving, coding, and project management. During my capstone project, I led a team to develop a mobile app, where I managed timelines, coordinated tasks, and ensured the project met user requirements."

- **Volunteer Work and Freelance Gigs Count!**
Volunteering or freelancing is a great way to build up your CV and show off real-world experience, even if it's unpaid. List any volunteer roles, side projects, or freelance gigs and the skills they helped you develop. Employers love initiative, and taking on extra responsibilities—especially if they're related to your target industry—demonstrates that you're proactive and eager to grow.

In fact, volunteer work can sometimes impress employers more than traditional paid roles because it shows a genuine passion and commitment to a cause. It proves that you're willing to contribute and go above and beyond without expecting a paycheck—something that can definitely set you apart from other candidates.
Example:

"As a volunteer coordinator for a local charity, I helped recruited and trained volunteers, and communicated with community partners to ensure the success of fundraising events. This hands-on experience allowed me to develop strong organizational and leadership skills, which are directly applicable to project management roles." or "Additionally, my freelance work designing marketing materials for small businesses gave me the opportunity to refine my creativity and attention to detail—skills I'm excited to apply in a full-time marketing position."

- **Add Extracurricular Activities to Show You're Well-Rounded**
  Hiring managers know that not all skills are learned in a classroom or on the job. Extracurricular activities can reveal a lot about your drive, adaptability, and team spirit. Were you part of a sports team, student council, a hobby group, or did you volunteer with a local organization? These experiences can say loads about your teamwork, leadership, time management, and communication skills.

  Extracurriculars matter because they demonstrate that you're not just focused on work or studies—they show you're able to balance multiple responsibilities, take initiative, and engage with others outside of a professional setting. Employers value candidates who bring a well-rounded, energetic approach to both life and work.

  Example:
  "As captain of my university's basketball team, I learned the importance of teamwork, strategic thinking, and maintaining focus under pressure. Managing practice

schedules and coordinating team events also honed my time management and leadership skills." or "Additionally, as a member of the student council, I collaborated with peers to organize campus-wide events, which sharpened my communication and organizational abilities. These experiences have equipped me with the interpersonal skills and work ethic to thrive in collaborative environments and take on leadership roles."

- **Let Your Personality Shine in a "Hobbies and Interests" Section**

  A bit of personality can make your CV feel more interesting and help you connect with hiring managers on a personal level. This can also be a way to align your interests with company culture. For instance, If you enjoy camping, travelling, or trying out new things, it suggests that you're adventurous, curious, and adaptable to new environments. If you write, paint, or create digital art, stress how your imaginative side can become handy in roles requiring problem-solving or innovation.

  Think of this section as your chance to show off a 3-dimensional personality that proves you're a genuine, well-rounded person. Don't be afraid to show your true colours—employers appreciate someone who feels authentic and isn't afraid to bring their full self to the table!

Example:
"Exploring different cultures through travel has fostered an open-minded approach to diverse perspectives—an asset in today's global workplace." "Reading historical non-fiction sharpens my analytical skills, helping me spot patterns and think critically." or "As a weekend soccer player, I'm dedicated to teamwork and strategic problem-solving."

The points above show that, even if you don't have a fancy job title yet, you can still show off a personality that's got layers—kind of like an onion, but less tear-jerking. You've got a global outlook, brainy analysis skills, and a knack for teamwork that'll make you look like a superstar in any workplace.

- **Show You're a Fast Learner**
  Employers love candidates who are eager to learn and can pick up new skills faster than you can say "Google it." Especially for fresh graduates or those with little working experience, showing that you're willing and able to learn quickly is crucial. Think about it—everyone starts somewhere, but the key is being open to learning and adapting on the job. Whether you're picking up a new software, mastering a complex task, or learning the ropes of office etiquette (like when it's okay to take the last donut), proving that you're a fast learner signals to employers that you're ready to grow into the role—even if you don't have years of experience. Plus, it shows you won't panic when faced with something you've never done before. After all, if you can survive your first year of

university without setting the kitchen on fire, you can definitely tackle a new challenge at work!

Example:

"Committed to continuous learning, I recently taught myself graphic design using online courses, mastering tools like Canva and Adobe Express to create professional visuals in just a few weeks. This experience demonstrates my ability to quickly adapt to new challenges, acquire skills independently, and apply them effectively."

A Sample CV Format

CV of Emily Smith

Core Competencies/Skills

Commercial Awareness
Strategic Planning & Execution
Consultative B2B selling
Communication & Presentation
Interpersonal Skills
Collaborative Team Player
Can-do Attitude
Stakeholder Management
Account Management
Market Research & Analysis

INTERESTS AND HOBBIES

Reading & Writing
Live Music
Movies & Drama
Hiking
Tennis
Traveling
International Relations

EDUCATION

Bachelor's degree
B. So. Sc. in Business Administration
University of xxxxxxxxx

PERSONAL SUMMARY

A results-driven leader in business development and account management, with a strong track record in market analysis, strategic planning, consultative B2B sales, and stakeholder engagement. Skilled at fostering key relationships and aligning organisational objectives through collaboration with senior stakeholders, including government bodies and industry partners. Now looking to apply versatile expertise in driving sales targets, business growth and client relations in a dynamic role within the industrial printing solutions sector.

WORKING EXPERIENCE

Job Title   January 2022 – Present
Company Name
[Description of Company]

Key Responsibilities:
- Identify and pursue new opportunities by analyzing market trends and understanding the pressing needs of the industry, and help them engage with the mainstream education sector for mutual benefits.
- Advise senior leadership of the organization on engagement strategies, supporting strategic decision-making on high-value initiatives and identifying areas for growth.
- Lead the development and execution of engagement programs aimed at capturing new business prospects and addressing industry demands, strengthening partnerships with key stakeholders including government bodies and diverse industry groups.
- Proactively manage stakeholder outreach initiatives, utilizing market intelligence to uncover growth areas and address critical industry concerns, leading to enhanced service delivery and operational improvements.
- Build and maintain strong relationships with external partners, industry organizations, and government agencies, using market insights to inform strategic decisions and develop new business channels.
- Develop proactive issues management strategies to mitigate risks, address media enquiries, and maintain the organization's reputation while pursuing growth opportunities.
- Provide expert advice to senior executives on industry engagement and market trends, ensuring the organisation remains at the forefront of emerging opportunities and industry developments.
- Monitor market trends and identify business growth opportunities

Key Achievements:
- Proactively identified and converted numerous opportunities into tangible business growth, significantly enhancing the organization's revenue streams.
- Engaged with diverse industries, successfully expanding the organization's reach by recruiting new members from untapped sectors.

LANGUAGE

English (Full Professional Proficiency)

Mandarin (Native)

OTHER INFORMATION

Right to Live, Study, and Work in the UK

A full, clean UK Driving Licence

REFERENCES

Available Upon Request

CONTACT

Address: xxxxxxxxxxxxxx

Mobile: xxxxxxxxxxx

Email: xxxxxxxx@gmail.com

- Cultivated and strengthened relationships with existing members, fostering significant growth in stakeholder partnerships and collaboration.
- Implemented market-driven strategies that bolstered the organisation's influence, establishing its leadership and enhancing brand visibility.

Title   **December 2005 – December 2022**
Company Name
[Description of Company]

Key Responsibilities:
- Conduct comprehensive market research using various channels, including attending industry events and participating as a keynote speaker in conferences and seminars to identify new markets and prospects.
- Drive new business initiatives and provide leadership in developing strategies for maximizing clients' full potential.
- Nurture existing C-suite relationships and find new ways to develop existing enterprise accounts.
- Manage and empower a staff team with professional knowledge, intellectual curiosity, and customer focus to achieve KPIs and improve service level.
- Facilitate discussions with enterprise clients, focusing on areas such as organizational transformation, business growth, and performance improvement.
- Prepare and present tailored proposals to address client needs, conducting successful contract negotiations with new clients.
- Monitor quantitative and qualitative analysis to identify concise problem areas and design effective solutions for enterprise clients that align with their evolving business and organizational needs.
- Consolidate the findings from the analysis and present a plan to clients to implement the recommended solutions.
- Create, implement, and review budgets, forecasts, and business growth plans.

Key Achievements:
- Pitched and won over 120 new enterprise accounts from a wide range of industries
- Completed over 300 cross-industries and/or cross-cultural projects
- Established a clear vision, fostering a mindset shift to embrace change throughout the organization
- Created a high standard, high performance, and high accountability company culture to grow all aspects of the business in unison
- Managed an annual revenue in excess of £800k

Chapter 3
Why Bother with a Cover Letter? Here's Why!

Think of your CV as the facts, and your cover letter as the why behind those facts. This is your opportunity to connect your experience to their needs. Show them you're not just qualified—you're tailor-made for the role.

Studies show that less than half of job applicants even bother to send one—so if you do, congratulations—you're already ahead of the pack! Hiring managers notice this effort, which can help you stand out in a crowded applicant pool.

Align with the Company's Culture

Hiring managers aren't just looking for someone who can do the job—they're looking for someone who gets the company's vibe. A cover letter also lets you show your alignment with the company's mission and culture, which hiring managers love. Tailoring it to the company's goals or values is like the cherry on top—it shows you've done your homework and care about the job.

If the job is about efficiency or growth, share a story about how you've tackled those challenges. Applying for a nonprofit like The Nature Conservancy? Show off your passion by talking about the time you organized a community beach cleanup or led a tree-planting initiative. Suddenly, you're not just another applicant—you're someone who genuinely cares.

Let's say you're applying for a project management gig at a tech giant like Google. Sure, your CV lists your experience managing teams and nailing deadlines, but your cover letter is where you can say, "Hey, remember that time I led a project for a startup that not only finished early but also came in under budget? Oh, and it boosted customer satisfaction by 30%? Yeah, that's me."

Tackle the Awkward Stuff

A good cover letter can also do some damage control. Got a weird gap in your work history? Made a career switch? This is your chance to explain why that time you took off to travel the world or go back to school actually made you a better fit for the job.

For instance, you could say, *"During my year off, I backpacked through Southeast Asia, where I honed my skills in budgeting and project planning — skills I put to use when I returned and successfully managed a $200,000 marketing campaign."* It's like writing your own plot twist — "Yes, I took a year off, but it taught me so much about time management (and surviving off street food in five different countries)."

Show Off Your Communication Skills

Even if writing isn't in the job description, clear communication is a superpower in almost any role. If you can craft a few sentences that don't make someone yawn—or worse, hit delete—you've already shown off a skill that's pure gold.

Case in point: I once wrote a cover letter to the Sales Director at one of the magnificent 7 to introduce myself. Now, here's the kicker—I had zero software or technology sales experience. Nada.

Zilch. But I still got the job. Curious (and maybe a little cocky), I asked him why he hired me. His answer? "Because the first sentence of your cover letter caught my eye."
So, there you have it: proof that one well-written line can change your life. Who needs industry experience when you've got the power of words, right?

For instance, if you're applying for a sales role, you could write: *"In my previous position, I revamped our internal communication strategy, leading to a 20% increase in team productivity."*

See? You're not just qualified—you're clear, concise, and compelling!

Stand Out with Creativity

If you're applying for a creative role, like graphic design at Adobe, your cover letter is the ultimate playground. Share a quirky story about designing an ad campaign that went viral or how a logo you created helped a nonprofit land a major grant. Creativity isn't just about what you've done—it's about how you present it. Make it memorable!

End with Enthusiasm

Don't let your cover letter fizzle out—end on a high note that leaves them buzzing about you. Whether you're excited to meet the team, eager to tackle your first project, or ready to bring fresh ideas to the table, let your enthusiasm shine. Try wrapping up with something like:

"I'm genuinely excited about the opportunity to bring my unique skills to your team and can't wait to discuss how we can drive results together!"

A dash of energy can go a long way, and it might just move your application to the top of the pile.

This is especially important if your experience isn't a perfect match for the job requirements or if you're just starting out. Don't let that stop you! Use the end of your cover letter to show employers that you're eager to learn, passionate about their mission, and committed to growing with the team for the long haul—not just looking to job-hop to the next opportunity.

Something like this could seal the deal:

"While I may not have direct experience in [specific area], I'm excited to bring my adaptability and dedication to the role. Your mission to [state company mission] resonates deeply with me, and I would be honored to contribute and grow as part of your team."

Show them your drive, your appreciation for the opportunity, and your willingness to go all in. Trust me, employers love someone who's genuinely invested—it's tempting for them to say, "Let's give this person a shot!"

The Bottom Line

Use the cover to tell your story, highlight your passion, and prove you're not just a good fit, but the perfect fit. With a little creativity and a lot of enthusiasm, your dream job might just be one well-crafted cover letter away.

Example 1: Corporate Internship

Subject: Application for Corporate Internship Position

Dear [Hiring Manager's Name],

I'm writing to express my excitement about the Corporate Internship opportunity at [Company Name]. As a business administration student at [University Name], I have developed a strong foundation in project management, communication, and data analysis, and I am eager to apply my skills in a corporate environment. After learning more about your company's innovative approach and commitment to nurturing young talent, I'm confident that my background aligns perfectly with the position.

During a recent internship with [Previous Company], I assisted with the coordination of cross-departmental projects, helping to streamline processes and improve team efficiency. My strong organizational skills and attention to detail enabled me to manage multiple tasks simultaneously. I'm particularly drawn to [Company Name]'s focus on growth and its mission to empower employees, which matches my own drive for continuous learning and improvement.

I'm eager to expand my knowledge and gain hands-on experience in the corporate world. This internship would be an invaluable opportunity for growth, and I'm committed to taking on new challenges to develop both professionally and personally.

Thank you for considering my application.

Best regards,
[Your Name]
[Your Contact Information]

Example 2: Data Analyst

Subject: Data Analyst Application

Dear [Hiring Manager's Name],

I am thrilled to apply for the Data Analyst position at [Company Name], as advertised. With a degree in statistics from [University Name], hands-on experience in data visualization, and a strong passion for turning raw data into actionable insights, I believe I can bring both technical expertise and creative problem-solving skills to your team.

In my most recent internship at [Previous Company], I worked closely with a team of analysts to collect, clean, and analyze large datasets, uncovering trends that directly contributed to more informed business decisions. One of my proudest accomplishments was creating a data dashboard that tracked customer behavior and identified key opportunities for increasing customer retention by 15%. I'm excited about the chance to bring this experience to your company and help drive similar results.

What excites me most about [Company Name] is your focus on leveraging data to solve real-world problems. I'm confident my analytical skills and ability to work collaboratively will be valuable assets to your team.

Thank you for considering my application. I appreciate your time and consideration, and I'm looking forward to the possibility of joining your team.

Sincerely,
[Your Name]
[Your Contact Information]

Example 3: Administrative Assistant

Subject: Application for Administrative Assistant Position

Dear [Hiring Manager's Name],

I am excited to apply for the Administrative Assistant position at [Company Name]. With [X years] of experience in administrative support, I am eager to bring my organizational skills and enthusiasm to your team.

In my previous role at [Previous Company], I managed complex calendars, coordinated travel arrangements, and streamlined office workflows, resulting in a 20% increase in team efficiency. I also took pride in handling confidential correspondence and ensuring that deadlines were met without fail—all while maintaining a positive, can-do attitude.

One of my key achievements was implementing a digital filing system that reduced document retrieval time by 50% and improved team collaboration. By introducing process improvements and staying on top of ever-changing priorities, I was able to help the team stay focused and productive.

What draws me to [Company Name] is your commitment to [innovation, teamwork, or customer service]. I am passionate about creating organized, supportive environments that empower teams to excel, and I'd love the opportunity to bring that energy to your office.

Thank you for considering my application. I look forward to the opportunity to discuss how I can contribute to your team.

Sincerely,
[Your Full Name]
[Your Contact Information]

Example 4: Marketing Manager

Subject 4: Marketing Manager Application

Dear [Hiring Manager's Name],

I'm excited to apply for the Marketing Manager position at [Company Name], as I believe my experience in developing strategic marketing campaigns and driving growth aligns perfectly with your company's vision.

Having spent the past three years at [Previous Company], leading a team of marketers and overseeing the execution of digital marketing strategies, I'm eager to bring my skills in project management, team leadership, and data-driven decision-making to your innovative team.

One of my proudest achievements was leading a marketing campaign for [Company Name] that resulted in a 30% increase in lead generation within six months. By leveraging targeted social media ads, email marketing, and content creation, we had improved our brand awareness by 25%—showcasing my ability to translate strategy into tangible outcomes.

I'd love to bring my passion for marketing and my experience in managing teams to contribute to your company's continued success. Thank you for considering my application.

I look forward to the opportunity to discuss how my background can support your marketing efforts and help take your brand to the next level.

Best regards,
[Your Full Name]
[Your Contact Information]

Example 5: Product Engineer

Subject: Application for Product Engineer Position

Dear [Hiring Manager's Name],

I am thrilled to apply for the Product Engineer position at [Company Name]. With a solid background in product design and development, coupled with a passion for innovation, I am eager to contribute my expertise to your dynamic team.

In my previous role at [Previous Company], I spearheaded the design and optimization of [specific product or system], which reduced manufacturing costs by 20% and improved performance reliability by 30%. By collaborating closely with cross-functional teams, I ensured that product development aligned seamlessly with customer needs and industry standards.

One of my proudest accomplishments involved leading the redesign of [specific project or component], which not only streamlined production but also enhanced user satisfaction. Leveraging tools such as [specific software or technology] and my proficiency in [specific skill], I was able to resolve complex technical challenges while delivering results ahead of schedule. The redesign reduced production time by 15% and decreased operational costs by 20%, Additionally, customer satisfaction scores improved by 6% following the implementation, reflecting the positive impact of the enhanced user experience.

What excites me most about [Company Name] is your commitment to [specific company value or innovation focus]. I am inspired by the opportunity to contribute to [specific project or initiative they're known for] and to be part of a team that pushes the boundaries of what's possible.

Thank you for considering my application. I would welcome the chance to discuss how my skills in product engineering, problem-solving, and innovation can support your goals and drive continued success.

Best regards,
[Your Full Name]
[Your Contact Information]

Chapter 4
Beyond the Basics: Innovative Places to Start Your Job Search

Sticking to the usual job boards is like always ordering plain cheese pizza—sure, it's reliable, but come on, where's the adventure? You're missing out on the pineapple-and-bacon combos of the job world—the ones that sound a little unusual but turn out to be exactly what you've been craving. The truth is, some of the juiciest roles never make it to the big platforms. They're snapped up faster than free samples at Costco, thanks to insider tips, word-of-mouth referrals, or low-key community postings that only the savvy job seeker can uncover.

By stepping out of the mainstream, you're giving yourself the chance to find those hidden gems. Think of it like treasure hunting but without the pirate hat (unless that's your thing). Maybe you send a bold, personalized email to that cool startup you found on Instagram. Or perhaps you spend an evening scrolling through niche forums where people in your industry hang out and share opportunities. These little detours from the standard job search can lead you straight to a role that screams dream job.

And let's not forget—employers love gutsy, creative candidates who think outside the box. Show them you're not just following the crowd by saying, "Oh, I found this job on a Reddit thread," and watch their eyebrows raise in impressed surprise. Taking the road less traveled isn't just smart; it makes you memorable.

Now, let's break it down one step at a time, starting with where you should look and how to make these bold moves work for you.

1. Job Platforms: Your Digital Marketplace

Job platforms are like the buffet of the career world—there's something for everyone, but knowing where to look and what to pile on your plate is key. From all-encompassing giants like LinkedIn and Indeed to niche gems like AngelList and Behance, each platform offers unique opportunities if you know how to use them strategically. Here's a breakdown of the best platforms and pro tips for maximizing your success on each.

LinkedIn: The Professional Playground

LinkedIn is more than just a place to flex your accomplishments. It's a hub for networking, job searching, and even subtle self-promotion.

How to Use It:
- Optimize Your Profile: Use a professional photo (ditch the selfies), write a punchy headline, and sprinkle keywords from job descriptions into your "About" section.

- Example: Instead of "Experienced sales professional," go for "Results-driven sales expert specializing in B2B solutions."

- Leverage the Job Search Tool: Use filters like location, industry, and job type to refine your search. Keywords like "remote marketing coordinator" or "entry-level software developer" can save you hours of scrolling.

- Engage with Content: Comment on posts, share relevant articles, or even post your own thoughts about your industry. This boosts your visibility.

- Pro Tip: When you apply for a job, message the hiring manager directly. Example: "Hi Alex, I saw your opening for a Product Manager. Your focus on innovation aligns perfectly with my experience, and I'd love to connect!"

Indeed: The Job Board for All Seasons

Indeed is the Swiss Army knife of job platforms. Whether you're exploring entry-level roles or high-paying gigs, you'll find it here.

How to Use It:
- Set Up Alerts: Don't waste time refreshing. Create alerts for specific roles like "graphic designer Los Angeles" to get updates straight to your inbox.

- Read Reviews: Check company ratings and salary insights to ensure the role aligns with your expectations.

- Tailor Your Applications: Use the job description to tweak your resume and cover letter. Indeed's platform often rewards customized applications with higher visibility to employers

Glassdoor: Research Before You Apply

Glassdoor is part job board, part snoop fest. It's where you go to find out if that "dynamic work environment" means bean bags and snacks or unpaid overtime.

How to Use It:
- Research Salaries: Know your worth before you apply. Use the salary tools to see what others in similar roles are earning.

- Check Company Reviews: Look for trends—if multiple employees mention poor management, it's a red flag.

- Browse Job Listings: Apply directly through the site, but make sure you've done your homework first.

AngelList: For Startup Stars

If you're dreaming of being part of the next big thing, AngelList is your spot. It's tailored to startup roles, especially in tech and creative industries.

How to Use It:
- Create a Standout Profile: Highlight your skills, past projects, and what you're looking for in a role. Example: "Passionate developer with a love for building intuitive apps in React. Seeking a remote role in an agile team."

- Apply in Bulk: AngelList allows you to apply to multiple jobs with one click.

- Direct Messaging: Found a startup you love? Message the founder directly. It's common in the startup world and shows initiative.

Creative Platforms: Behance and Dribbble

For designers, illustrators, and other visual creatives, these platforms double as portfolios and job boards.

How to Use Them:
- Keep Your Portfolio Updated: Showcase your best work and write brief descriptions about the process behind each project.

- Engage with the Community: Like and comment on others' work to build connections.

- Use Job Boards: Many companies post creative roles here, often looking for freelance or remote talent.

Remote-Specific Platforms: We Work Remotely and Remote.co

The remote work revolution is here, and these platforms are leading the charge.

How to Use Them:
- Narrow Down Time Zones: Apply for roles that fit your schedule to avoid awkward 3 a.m. meetings.

- Highlight Remote-Friendly Skills: Show off your ability to self-manage, communicate effectively, and use collaborative tools like Slack or Zoom.

College Job Boards and Handshake: For the Fresh Grads

If you're just starting out, college career centers and platforms like Handshake are treasure troves for internships and entry-level roles.

How to Use Them:
- Attend Career Fairs: Many colleges host these through Handshake. Dress sharp, bring a polished resume, and practice your elevator pitch.

- Apply Early: Competition is fierce for graduate roles, so get your applications in as soon as listings go live.

- Tailor your CV to match the keywords in the job description. Many companies use AI to filter candidates, so you want your resume to hit the algorithm's sweet spot.

2. Targeting Companies Directly: Think Out of the Box

Sometimes, the best jobs aren't advertised. It's like an exclusive club—you just need to know where to look (and how to charm the bouncer).

How to Start:
- Create a hit list of companies you admire. Are you a sustainability fanatic? Go for eco-conscious startups. Tech enthusiast? Hunt down companies that just landed funding—they're basically waving a "we're hiring" flag. A quick Google search for "Top 10 Sustainable Companies in London" will give you a solid lineup. Jot them down, grab a cup of coffee, and start scoping out their Careers pages like you're on a treasure hunt.

- Email your dream employer even if there's no job posting. Because why not? Worst case, they ignore you. Best case? They think, "Wow, this person has guts—and a killer email game."

The Real-Life Power of Shooting Your Shot:
- True story: Once, I sent an unsolicited application to one of the "Magnificent Seven". Not through HR—because let's face it, HR might've tossed my CV into the "cabbage bin" (aka the trash)—but directly to the Country Manager. I had zero experience in IT, but I focused on what I did bring to the table: entrepreneurial spirit, leadership chops, and top-notch stakeholder management skills.

- Guess what? The Country Manager loved it. He found my approach bold, my skills transferable, and my story compelling. If I'd gone the HR route, I probably would've gotten a polite rejection email (if I was lucky). Instead, I got a shot at impressing someone who gets the bigger picture. See the example below:

Subject: Enthusiast Ready to Contribute

Hi [Country Manager's Name],

I'm [Your Name], and I'm reaching out because I'm excited about the opportunity to contribute to [Company Name], the market leader in [industry]. Although I haven't worked directly in [industry], my experience in [relevant skill/industry] has equipped me with a unique skill set that could add value to your team.

Here's how I can make an impact:

1) <u>Stakeholder Management:</u> At [Previous Company], I successfully led cross-functional teams, aligning diverse departments towards a common goal, which resulted in [specific achievement].

2) <u>Strategic Leadership:</u> I've developed and implemented strategies that boosted sales by 35%, showing my ability to drive results.

3) <u>Innovation:</u> Spearheaded a digital transformation, engaging the entire staff in the process.

I'm eager to bring my skills to a market leader like [Company Name] and would love to connect about potential opportunities.

Thanks for your time—I look forward to hearing from you!

Sincerely,
[Your Name]
[Your Contact Information]

The moral of the true story: Sometimes it's not about checking all the boxes; it's about finding someone who sees you as the out-of-the-box candidate they didn't know they needed.

Don't let the "no job posting" excuse stop you. Aim for the decision-makers, charm them with your enthusiasm, and show them why you're worth a second look. Remember, fortune favors the bold—and in this case, the well-prepared and slightly cheeky.

So if you are a designer, just send a message directly to the owner of a design studio—*"Hey, your work is fire! Any openings on your team?"* What's the worst that could happen? They ignore you? No biggie, on to the next.

3. Uni & College Placement Centers: Hidden Gems

If you're fresh out of school, placement centers are your secret weapon. These often-overlooked hubs offer:

- Job boards with postings specifically for graduates.
- Workshops on CV writing, interview prep, and networking.
- Connections with alumni who've been there, done that, and might be hiring.

Example: Your college career center offers mock interview sessions. You sign up, practice your "Why should we hire you?" spiel, and walk into your first interview ready to conquer.

4. Old-School Networking (Yes, It Still Works!)

Sometimes, all you need is a good chat over coffee. Reach out to people in your network:
- Former classmates
- Former colleagues or managers
- Friends who work in your industry
- LinkedIn connections with interesting job titles

Reaching Out to a Classmate:
You spot a classmate from university who has landed a job at a company you're interested in. You message them:

"Hey [Name], I saw you're working at [Company]—that's awesome! I've been following their work, and I'd love to hear more

about your experience there. Any chance they're looking for someone in [Your Role]?"

Reaching Out to a Former Manager:
You notice a former manager has just moved to a new company. You reach out:

"Hi [Manager's Name], congrats on your new role at [Company]! I've always admired your leadership and would love to hear about how things are going there. Do you know if they're hiring for [Your Role] or similar positions?"

Reaching Out to a Former Coworker
You see a post from an old coworker celebrating their promotion. Reply with a genuine interest:

"Congrats on your new role! Your company sounds amazing—do you know if they're hiring for [Your Role]?"

5. Career Fairs and Events

Look for job fairs, industry meet-ups, or seminars. Job fairs are the speed-dating events of the employment world. Dress to impress, bring your CV, and have a quick elevator pitch ready that highlights your experience and career goals.

If you're at an engineering job fair, say, *"Hi, I'm [Name]. I specialize in [your expertise] and am passionate about solving [specific problem]. I'd love to know more about the opportunities at your company."*

After attending a tech expo and stumble upon a startup hiring developers, you chat with the founder, exchange business cards, and send a follow-up email that lands you an interview, see an example below:

"It was great meeting you at [Event Name]! I enjoyed learning more about [Company Name] and the exciting projects you're working on. I'm very interested in the developer role we discussed and believe my skills in [key skill/experience] would be a great fit. I've attached my CV for your reference and would love the chance to discuss how I can contribute to your team."

6. Get Social with Social Media

Social media is an untapped goldmine for job hunting. By following the right hashtags, connecting with industry pros, and actively engaging, you can uncover opportunities and network with ease. Start posting and engaging—you never know where it might lead!

Follow Industry Hashtags
Hashtags like #HiringNow, #JobOpening, and #TechJobs are your ticket to job gold. Forget scrolling through endless cat videos—start scrolling for opportunities!

Example: You spot a tweet about a developer role under #TechJobs. You reply, "I'm your next developer—let's chat!" (Confident, right?)

Connect with Companies and Leaders
Follow your dream companies and industry bigwigs like you're stalking the latest celebrity gossip. Companies often post openings in their stories or tweets—be ready to pounce!

Example: You reply to a company's Instagram story: "Your work is amazing! Any chance you're hiring in [Your Role]?" (Might as well slide into those DMs with style!)

Join Groups and Forums

Get in on industry-specific groups or Twitter chats. It's like a secret club, but with job leads and no awkward handshakes.

Example: You join a #MarketingJobs chat and drop a comment like, "This role sounds like my dream job—let's talk about how I can boost your content strategy!"

7. Build your Personal Brand

To elevate your job search to the next level, don't just stick to browsing job platforms. Sometimes, the key to standing out is getting employers and recruiters to come to you. Imagine being offered an interview without even applying—that's the power of a strong personal brand. Here's how you can make it happen:

Manage Your LinkedIn Network

LinkedIn isn't just a glorified online resume. It's a powerful tool for building your personal brand, staying informed about industry trends, and opening doors to job opportunities.

Managing your LinkedIn network strategically is like nurturing a thriving garden—it requires consistent care and attention, but the results can be incredibly rewarding. Here's how to cultivate it effectively:

a) Craft a Standout Profile

First thing first, your LinkedIn profile is your online billboard, so make it compelling:

Professional Photo: Use a high-quality, approachable headshot.

Headline: Highlight your unique value, not just your job title. Think: "Helping companies grow through innovative marketing solutions" rather than "Marketing Manager".

About Section: Tell your story. Share your passions, skills, and what drives you in a conversational tone. Use keywords relevant to your industry to improve searchability.

Experience: Don't just list roles; showcase accomplishments with metrics, if possible ("Increased sales by 30% in 12 months").

Skills & Endorsements: Add skills relevant to your industry and request endorsements from colleagues or clients.

Regular Update: Finally, don't forget to update your profile and use keywords relevant to your target roles so that others can easily find and connect with you.

b) Develop a Content Strategy

Share value-driven content to establish yourself as a thought leader:

Post Regularly: Share insights, articles, and opinions on industry trends. Aim for 1-2 posts per week.
Write Articles: Think blog, not diary. Save your "My dog ate my Wi-Fi cable" saga for Facebook.

Engage with Others: Engage regularly by liking, commenting on, or sharing insightful posts to stay visible. Add comments on posts that aren't just "Great post!" That's like giving someone a high-five and walking away.

Showcase Achievements: Humblebrag, but with class. "Excited to share that I increased revenue by 30% last quarter!"—no need to mention the celebratory pizza party that followed.

Congratulate connections: Always congratulate connections' new jobs or anniversaries, secretly you're wondering if they're hiring.

Become a content machine: Share cool insights, trends, or even a funny anecdote about your industry. After posting a thought-provoking article on LinkedIn, next thing you know, a recruiter asks for your CV.

c) Grow Your Connections

Expanding your LinkedIn connections is all about being strategic and proactive.

Start by reaching out to colleagues, classmates, and industry peers you already know. Then, send personalized connection requests to professionals in your field—like recruiters, hiring managers, or thought leaders—explaining why you'd like to connect.

Personalized Invites: Don't be that person who sends a blank request. That's like yelling, "Hi!" from across the street and then running away.

Join Groups: Think of it like a high school clique, but professional. Find your tribe—minus the cafeteria drama. Join LinkedIn groups related to your industry and participate in discussions to network with like-minded professionals.

Reconnect: Send messages like, "Hey, remember me from accounting? We bonded over terrible coffee at that work conference."

d) Be Authentic

No one wants to connect with a robot—or someone who sounds like they're selling timeshares in Florida:

Share real stories. Like the time you accidentally sent an email to the entire company but turned it into a lesson on attention to detail.

Avoid jargon overload. Nobody wants to "circle back" to your "paradigm-shifting value proposition." Just... no.

Don't fake it. Unless you're a magician, in which case, congrats, your LinkedIn is already magical.

e) Use LinkedIn Tools

LinkedIn is like a buffet—you've got to use the tools to get your money's worth (even if it's free):

Creator Mode: Activate it if you want to be a LinkedIn influencer. Yes, that's a thing.

Hashtags: They're like seasoning. Use a little, not the whole shaker. Nobody likes a #HashtagExplosion.

Analytics: It's like a report card for your posts. Just don't cry over low views like you did with your SAT scores.

f) Share Your Skills and Work

Post about your awesome projects, so recruiters can't ignore your brilliance. Use hashtags like #OpenToWork so it's obvious you're ready to rock and roll.

Example: You share your latest design on Instagram and tag it #OpenToWork. Boom, a recruiter slides into your DMs about a new position. (You're basically a social media superstar now.)

g) Add Value

Be the person everyone wants in their corner—like a good Wi-Fi connection:
Share job leads. Nothing says "networking MVP" like "Hey, I thought of you for this role!"

Offer mentorship. Or at least pretend to know the answer until you can Google it.

Highlight others' achievements. Bonus points if it makes you look humble, too.

h) Be Consistent

Rome wasn't built in a day, and neither is a killer LinkedIn brand. Post, engage, repeat. Consistency is key—just like showing up to Starbucks and pretending you're not addicted to the Pumpkin Spice Latte.

Create an Online Presence

In today's digital age, your online presence is often the first impression employers and recruiters will have of you—sometimes even before they've seen your CV. So, why not take control of that narrative and showcase your skills, personality, and passion in a way that truly stands out?

Step 1: Build Your Digital Home

Create a personal website or online portfolio where you can display your work, especially if you're in a creative or technical field. Think of it as your virtual business card—but way cooler. Include sections like:

- A professional bio to tell your story.
- Highlights of your best work, whether it's design projects, coding samples, writing clips, or even event photos.
- Testimonials or recommendations from past colleagues, clients, or mentors.
- Contact details or a form that makes it easy for potential employers to reach out.

Step 2: Share Your Expertise

Start a blog or vlog to share your thoughts on industry trends, challenges, or personal experiences. This not only positions you as an engaged and knowledgeable professional but also boosts your visibility. Recruiters searching for insights might stumble upon your content and be impressed by your perspective.

Example: Write a blog post titled "5 Trends Transforming [Your Industry] and How I'm Ready for Them." Share it widely on LinkedIn, Twitter, or niche forums to spark conversations. Bonus: It doubles as a conversation starter in interviews!

Step 3: Add a Personal Touch

Record a short video introducing yourself and your career goals. Keep it professional but authentic. Share your passion for what you do and what excites you about your industry. Platforms like

LinkedIn or even TikTok (for creative industries) are great for this. A face-to-face connection—even a virtual one—can leave a lasting impression.

Step 4: Stay Active and Engaged

An online presence isn't "set it and forget it." Regularly update your site, post on social media, or engage in industry discussions. Share articles, comment on trends, or give shoutouts to projects that inspire you. This keeps you visible and relevant.

Why It Works:

By crafting a strong online presence, you're not just waiting for opportunities to find you—you're actively showcasing yourself to the world. Employers value proactive, engaged candidates, and a standout digital presence makes you impossible to ignore.

Who knows? Your dream job might just slide into your DMs!

Use Niche Job Boards and Communities

Why It Works:

Specialized job boards and professional communities attract exactly the kind of recruiters and employers looking for talent in your field. Instead of competing with thousands of generic applicants, you're getting in front of the right people.

Pro Tips:

Join online forums, discussion groups, or Slack channels where industry professionals hang out. You never know when an employer or recruiter might be lurking.

Engage consistently. Post your work, share ideas, or respond to questions. It's like attending a never-ending networking event, but with better snacks (because you're at home).

Example:
If you're in tech, sign up for GitHub. Share your code, contribute to open-source projects, and get noticed by recruiters scouting for talent.

If you're in the creative world, Behance is your playground. Showcase your portfolio, connect with other creatives, and stay on the radar of companies looking for fresh design talent.

The trick is to be visible, valuable, and consistent. In these communities, your dream job might find you!

# Chapter 5
Research the Company – The Key to Interview Success!

So, you've landed an interview—congrats! But before you roll in and wow them with your experience, there's one crucial step you *must* take: researching the company. Trust me, walking into an interview without knowing key details about the company is like going on a first date and not even knowing their name. You're not setting yourself up for success.

But don't worry, you don't need to know the CEO's favorite pizza topping! Here's how to dig deep and get the inside scoop that will help you not only impress the hiring manager but also figure out if the company is really the right fit for you.

1. Start with the Basics – Mission & Vision

Before you even think about the interview, you've got to do your homework—especially when it comes to the company's mission and vision. Picture this: you're at the interview, and they ask, "What attracted you to our company?" and you freeze. You could say, "Uh, the free coffee?" or "The year-end bonus" but that won't win you any points. Instead, you can confidently say, "I love how your mission to promote sustainability really resonates with me. I've always wanted to work for a company that's committed to positive change." Boom. You just nailed it.

Why is this important? Because companies live and breathe their mission and vision. It's what drives their culture, goals, and even hiring decisions. If they're passionate about innovation, and you're a tech wizard, now you've got a shared passion to talk about. Your answers will align better with what they value, and that's how you show you've actually done your research, not just copied and pasted from LinkedIn.

2. Check Out Their Products and Services

Alright, you know the company's mission, but do you know what they actually do? You'd be surprised how many people walk into an interview knowing the company's slogan but have no clue what product or service they offer. Imagine saying, "So, what exactly do you guys sell?" Awkward.

Here's the deal: whether you're applying for a food delivery app or a fancy tech company, knowing their products is a huge plus. Say you're interviewing for a mobile app company, and you've actually downloaded their app (shocking, I know, but it's called effort), then you can go in with specific insights. "I noticed your app's interface is super user-friendly, but maybe adding a dark mode could improve user experience." Look at you—professional and insightful!

By being knowledgeable about their offerings, you're not just another resume on the pile. You're someone who's genuinely interested and has taken the time to learn about what they do. Bonus points if you can impress them with a product suggestion, but don't go overboard—let's not pretend you're their next product manager if you're just there for a marketing role!

3. Follow Their News and Updates

Imagine showing up to an interview and saying, "So, what's new with you guys?" Yeah, that's not going to impress anyone. But here's the secret: companies LOVE to talk about their recent achievements. They're like that friend who just got a new puppy and won't stop posting about it. Instead of awkwardly pretending you didn't see their latest accomplishments, dive in and make it part of the conversation.

Why is this important? Because it shows you're not just a resume with a face. You're someone who's actually paying attention to what they're up to. For instance, if they recently won an award for sustainability, you could casually drop, "I saw you won that sustainability award—pretty impressive! I've always been passionate about green initiatives, so that really caught my eye." Bam! Now you're a knowledgeable and eco-friendly superstar who cares about their mission.

This kind of info is like interview gold—free insight into what the company is proud of and what direction they're heading. It's your opportunity to show that you're not just applying to "any job"—you're applying to their job, and you've got the goods to back it up. Mentioning their latest achievements makes you look like you've done your homework (because you have), and it makes the interview feel more like a conversation and less like a creepy interrogation. So, go ahead, make them proud—they'll love you for it.

4. Stalk—Er, Follow Them on Social Media

In this digital age, companies are active on social media platforms like LinkedIn, Twitter, Instagram, and Facebook. Follow them! Not only will this give you a better sense of their brand voice and culture, but it'll also keep you in the loop about what's happening in real time.

5. Check Out Their Competitors

Understanding the competitive landscape is like knowing the playbook before the big game. Who are the company's biggest rivals? What makes them better or different? Knowing this will give you an edge in the interview. It's like being the only person in the room who's read the latest gossip on the competition. For example, if you're interviewing for a job at a clothing brand, you can confidently say, "I see you're competing with X and Y brands, but what really stands out about you is your commitment to sustainable fashion. I've worked in eco-friendly initiatives, and I'd love to bring that expertise to help you grow in this market." This shows you're not just another job seeker—you're a strategist who's aware of the big picture.

By understanding who they're up against, you can highlight how you'll help the company stay ahead of the pack. It's like being the underdog who's ready to take on the competition—just without the whole "Rocky training montage" part (unless you really want to, of course).

6. Understand Their Challenges

No company is perfect—if they were, they wouldn't need you. Every business has its challenges, and understanding these can turn you from just another applicant into the problem-solver they didn't know they needed. Research any struggles or areas where the company is looking to improve. It could be anything from updating their tech, navigating new markets, or tackling new regulations. Don't bring it up awkwardly, but use it to your advantage.

Let's say the company is expanding internationally, and you have global experience. You could say, "I saw your push to expand into international markets, and I'd love to bring my experience with global clients to help streamline that process." See? You're not just showing that you're a great fit—you're showing you're the answer to their prayers. It's like being the hero in an action movie, but instead of fighting bad guys, you're fighting inefficiency and market barriers. You'll be the first one they call when they need a solution—and who doesn't want to be the hero?

7. Look Up the Hiring Manager

Okay, don't go full Sherlock Holmes on them, but doing a little detective work on the hiring manager can make a huge difference. It's not just about finding out what they look like, but about understanding their background, interests, and professional vibe. If you know something about them—maybe they shared an article you're into or have worked in a field you admire—you can use that to build rapport during the interview.

For example, if you notice they're passionate about the same industry trends, you can casually say, "I saw on your LinkedIn that you're into [industry trend]. I've worked on similar projects, and it'd be great to hear your thoughts." This shows you've done your homework and makes the conversation more personal. It's all about making a connection. By showing interest in them, you're no longer just a candidate—you're someone who's genuinely engaged and ready to contribute.

8. Get the Inside Scoop—Employee Reviews

Glassdoor, Indeed, and other employee review sites can be a treasure trove of insights about what it's like to work at a company. While you should take some reviews with a grain of salt, recurring themes—whether positive or negative—are often worth noting. Are employees raving about the work-life balance? Or is there a pattern of comments about high turnover? This kind of research can help you prepare thoughtful questions to ask in the interview, like, "How does the company support employee growth?" or "What is the company's approach to work-life balance?"

9. Check Their Culture Fit

Finally, you get an interview, make sure that you are not walking into a culture shock! Company culture is a huge deal—it's like dating. You want to know if you're going to vibe with them long-term, or if it's just a temporary fling. Are they a fast-paced startup where everyone wears five hats and chugs energy drinks for breakfast? Or do they have a more chill, traditional vibe with 9-to-5 hours and a dress code that still includes ties (for some reason)?

Knowing the culture helps you determine if you'll fit in—because let's be real, you don't want to end up in an office where the only thing moving faster than your workload is the gossip. And it gives you the perfect opportunity to highlight how your personality and work style match. For example, if you're interviewing for a fast-paced, innovative company, you can say, "I thrive in dynamic environments, and I'm always up for tackling new challenges on the fly." Or if it's a more traditional setup, you might add, "I appreciate a structured environment where I can really focus on delivering consistent results."

Either way, being a culture match isn't just about fitting in—it's about knowing if you'll enjoy your time there. A great company culture means you won't dread waking up on Monday morning, and that's something worth researching.

In a nutshell

Researching the company isn't just about impressing the hiring manager—it's about making sure the company is the right fit for you. By diving into the company's values, challenges, and culture, you'll walk into the interview with confidence, ready to not only answer questions but also ask some killer ones of your own. So, grab your detective hat, do your homework, and show up to that interview ready to knock it out of the park!

I remember once I was sitting on the other side of the interview table, faced with two candidates who were equally qualified. It was a real coin toss—both had the skills, the experience, and the charm to match. And then Pete walked in. Oh, Pete. Not only did he come prepared, but the guy went full eagle-eye mode. He had researched our company so thoroughly I half-expected him to tell me where I left my car keys.

But wait—there's more. Pete waltzes in with a slick little presentation. Not some boring PowerPoint snooze-fest, no sir. This was a TED Talk-level breakdown of where we are, where we could go in the next decade, and exactly how we could crush it along the way. He even threw in a couple of pie charts! I didn't even know I liked pie charts.

By the end, I was so impressed I didn't just offer him the job—I practically slid the contract across the table with a bow on it. Let me tell you, there's always room on the team for someone who makes you think, Man, I wish I'd thought of that.

Chapter 6
Prepared for the Questions (and How Not to Sound Like a Robot!)

You know the drill—they're going to ask the classics: "Tell me about yourself," "Why do you want this job?" and "What's your biggest weakness?"

You don't need to have your answers tattooed on your arm, but a bit of practice doesn't hurt. Grab a friend or a mirror (less judgment from the mirror), and run through a few mock interviews. Bonus points if you can do it without cringing at the sound of your own voice.

Don't want to ask a friend for help or expert advice (sorry, Mom and Dad!), consider using interview prep tools to sharpen your skills. These nifty tools offer video lessons and mock interviews that let you record yourself and get instant feedback on your performance—think of it as your personal hype squad that points out your overuse of "um" and "like." Many candidates find this approach super effective because the feedback is specific and actionable. Some popular interview prep tools are: **Interviewing.io** (free for candidates, **Big Interview** (offers a free trial), and **Pramp** (free to use for peer-to-peer mock interviews).

Pro Tip: Don't rehearse so much that you end up sounding like you're reading from a script. You want to come across as prepared, not robotic. Remember, interviews are all about the vibes, and nobody vibes with a robot! And for the love of all things caffeinated, steer clear of memorizing corporate-sounding answers. Interviewers can sniff out a scripted response from a mile away. So, keep it genuine but polished!

Example 1: Why do you want to work here?

Oh, please don't say, "I applied to everything on Indeed faster than my Wi-Fi could handle." That kind of enthusiasm might sound like you're eager, but trust me—it screams, "I need a paycheck yesterday," and no hiring manager is charmed by desperation.

In fact, I once had an applicant give me this exact line. Guess what? I showed him the door before he could even finish telling me about his "vast experience" and "impressive strengths."

The lesson here? Desperation is a vibe no one wants to catch—especially not in the workplace. Employers want to know that you're interested in the job for the right reasons, like growth, challenge, and opportunity, not just because your phone bill is due.

So, keep it cool. Show enthusiasm, but save the "frenzied job-applying marathon" for your personal life. Hiring managers are looking for candidates who are excited about the role because it aligns with their skills and career goals—not because they're swiping right on every job listing like it's a dating app.

Instead, let's pump up the enthusiasm and show them why you're here for them. This is your chance to channel your inner fan and tell them why their company makes you want to throw on a branded T-shirt and do a happy dance.

Maybe you admire their mission—like, they're saving the planet or revolutionizing tech, and you're ready to sign up as the sidekick to their superhero. Or maybe the role feels like a perfect match for your strengths, where you can use your selling skills like a pro and wow their clients. Bonus points if you can sprinkle in how the position will help you grow, too—because hey, you're all about leveling up, right?

The formula to success is: genuine admiration for the company + how the role matches your strengths + why this is a win-win for both sides. Add a touch of humor (but not stand-up comedy), and you'll have them saying, "This is the person we need!"

Here are some examples showcasing how to tailor responses based on individual values and experiences:

- *"I'm drawn to your company's culture of collaboration and creativity. I thrive in environments where team members share ideas freely and encourage each other to think outside the box. I believe my experience in developing innovative marketing strategies will mesh well with your team-oriented approach, and I'm excited about the possibility of contributing to a workplace that values teamwork and diverse perspectives."*

- *"I'm really impressed by your focus on innovation and technology. As someone who has always been passionate about leveraging cutting-edge solutions to solve complex problems, I admire how your company leads the industry in developing groundbreaking products."*

- *"I want to work for your organization because I deeply resonate with your mission to create positive social impact. Your initiatives in community development align with my personal values and experiences. I have volunteered extensively in various nonprofit sectors, and I'm excited about the opportunity to use my skills in program management to help further your mission of uplifting underserved communities."*

- *"I'm excited about this opportunity because it aligns perfectly with my expertise in B2B consultative selling. I've always enjoyed building long-term relationships with clients, understanding their unique challenges, and delivering tailored solutions that create real value. I'm eager to contribute by driving sales and fostering partnerships that support your growth objectives."*

- *"I admire your company's commitment to integrity and transparency, values that I hold in high regard. In my previous roles, I've prioritized building trust with clients and stakeholders, which I believe is crucial for long-term success. I'm excited about the opportunity to work for a company that shares my values and strives for ethical business practices."*

- *"I've always had a passion for the healthcare industry, and your company stands out as a leader in providing innovative solutions that improve patient outcomes. I want to be part of an organization that is dedicated to making a real difference in people's lives. I'm excited about the opportunity to apply my skills in healthcare project management to contribute to your important work."*

Example 2: Asking about Your Weaknesses

Don't roll out the old, tired "I'm a perfectionist" unless you want to see their eyes glaze over. Instead, say something like, *"I tend to get caught up in details, but I've learned to manage that by setting clear deadlines."* It's honest, shows growth, and proves you've working on your weakness and got it under control.

Here are a few more answers that emphasize the principle of improvement:

- *"I've struggled with public speaking in the past, but I've been actively working on it by joining a local Toastmasters group. It's helped me build my confidence and communication skills."* This shows that you're aware of your weakness and are taking steps to improve.

- *"Time management has been a challenge for me, especially when juggling multiple projects. To tackle this, I've started using project management tools to prioritize tasks and keep myself on track."* This highlights your commitment to personal development and effective organization.

- *"I used to find it difficult to delegate tasks because I wanted everything to be done perfectly. However, I've realized that trusting my team leads to better results. Now, I make a conscious effort to delegate and support my colleagues, which has improved our overall productivity."* This illustrates that you've recognized a shortcoming and transformed it into a strength through collaboration.

- *"I used to hesitate when making decisions, worrying about getting everything just right. To overcome this, I've started focusing on gathering key information quickly and trusting my judgment to move forward. It's helped me make timely decisions without overthinking."* This shows you're proactive and have developed strategies to handle challenges effectively.

- *"Networking didn't come naturally to me—I used to feel out of place at events. But I've made an effort to attend more meetups and engage with people one-on-one. Over time, I've become more comfortable, and it's even led to some great professional connections."* This demonstrates self-awareness and your ability to push past discomfort for personal and professional growth.

Example 3: Solving Complex Problems with Various Stakeholders

You might get asked something like, *"Give an example of how you solved a complex problem by working with various stakeholders internally and externally?"* This is your time to show you're the *problem-solving superhero* they're looking for. Instead of just saying, "I collaborated with different teams," try:

- *"I was managing a project that involved multiple departments—marketing, product, and customer support. Each had conflicting priorities, so I organized weekly check-ins to align everyone. Externally, I coordinated with our suppliers to ensure we had the resources we needed. It wasn't easy, but by keeping communication clear and setting mutual goals, we successfully launched the product ahead of schedule."*

- *"I was tasked with improving a sales process that involved input from the sales team, IT, and legal. Each group had different priorities—sales wanted speed, IT focused on system limitations, and legal was all about compliance. I scheduled workshops to understand their needs, created a roadmap that balanced their concerns, and introduced a streamlined CRM workflow. By the end, not only did we reduce deal closure time by 20%, but we also had all departments on board and working harmoniously. Who knew bringing sales and legal together could feel like less of a cage fight?"*

- *"During a customer onboarding revamp, I had to manage expectations between the client, our internal teams (sales, product, and implementation), and a third-party vendor. Everyone had different ideas of what success looked like. I set up a shared project plan, ran bi-weekly alignment meetings, and kept all parties informed with clear updates. By coordinating timelines and expectations, we delivered a smoother onboarding experience, cut the go-live time in half, and earned a glowing testimonial from the client. It was a juggling act, but I didn't drop a single ball—or a stakeholder's trust."*

Boom—now you're showing you're not just a team player, but also a team wrangler.

Example 3: Leading a Team to Boost Revenue

Another popular one: *"How did you lead a team to achieve revenue growth?"* This isn't the time to be vague. Skip the "I motivated the team" line and go for:

- *"We were facing a dip in sales, so I led a brainstorming session with the sales and marketing teams to find out where we could improve. We identified a key customer pain point and created a targeted campaign around it. I also introduced a new incentive structure for the sales team, which boosted morale. Together, these strategies resulted in a 35% increase in revenue within six months."*

- *"My team were struggling to hit our quarterly revenue targets. I analyzed our sales data and noticed we weren't tapping into our existing client base for upselling opportunities. I organized training sessions to equip the team with consultative selling techniques and launched a client outreach campaign highlighting complementary services. Within three months, we turned things around, exceeding our target by 25% and creating a pipeline for future growth."*

- *"Our department was tasked with increasing subscription renewals, which were stuck at a 60% rate. I spearheaded a cross-functional effort with the customer success and marketing teams to create a proactive engagement plan. We introduced quarterly check-ins with clients, shared tailored success stories, and offered exclusive renewal incentives. Additionally, I monitored the team's progress through a dashboard to address challenges quickly. By the next quarter, our renewal rate jumped to 85%, significantly boosting our recurring revenue."*

By supporting your claims with figures and highlighting the process, you demonstrate that you're strategic and capable of delivering results.

Example 4: Handling Human Resources Nightmares

There's the classic: *"What's the most difficult human resources problem you've encountered, and how did you resolve it?"* Instead of glossing over with "I handled it professionally," be real:

- *"Two key team members were constantly clashing, disrupting the whole department. I met with each individually to understand their perspectives, then facilitated a mediation session to address the conflict. We established clear communication guidelines and accountability measures. Within weeks, their collaboration improved, and the team's performance rebounded, exceeding prior productivity levels."*

- *"Our team faced a high turnover rate due to unclear roles and inconsistent feedback. I implemented a structured onboarding process and set up regular one-on-one check-ins to provide clear expectations and address concerns early. Within six months, turnover dropped by 40%, and employee satisfaction scores increased significantly."*

- *"I managed a situation where an underperforming employee's attitude was demotivating the team. I conducted a candid yet supportive meeting to address the issues and provided a performance improvement plan with clear goals and timelines. With coaching and regular progress reviews, the employee not only improved but became a valuable contributor, restoring team morale."*

Now you're showing you've got the emotional intelligence and leadership skills to handle tough situations—and that's what they want to hear.

Example 5: Why leaving the Previous Company

Ah, the infamous *"Why Did You Leave Your Last Job?"* question—potentially a minefield, but don't panic! Let's navigate this together so you're fully prepared for this tricky query. First off, resist the urge to throw your previous company under the bus. Even if your boss made Miranda Priestly from *The Devil Wears Prada* look like a walk in the park, professionalism is key. On the flip side, a vague response like, "It was time for a change" won't impress anyone. Instead, craft an answer that showcases your growth and future aspirations while maintaining a positive tone.

Here's how to navigate this question gracefully and honestly, avoiding any traps along the way:

The Growth Opportunity - If you're moving on because you're looking for more responsibility, try something like: *"I learned a lot during my time there, but I felt like I had hit a ceiling in terms of growth. I'm excited about this opportunity because it offers new challenges and the chance to continue developing my skills in [specific area relevant to the new job]."*

Why It Works: You're showing that you're forward-thinking, driven, and eager to grow—plus, it shifts the focus to why this new role is such a great fit.

The Company Pivot - Maybe your last company changed direction, and it no longer aligned with your goals. In this case, you could say: *"My previous company went through some restructuring, and the role I was in became less focused on the areas I'm passionate about, like [insert skills here]. I'm looking for an opportunity where I can apply my strengths in [new company's focus]."*

Why It Works: You're being honest without badmouthing anyone. Plus, it shows you know what you want—and that you've done your homework on the company you're interviewing with.

The Relocation - Sometimes, it's just about geography. If that's your case, something simple like: *"I relocated to [new city], and unfortunately, the role couldn't transition with me. I'm really excited to explore new opportunities here, especially at a company like [insert company name]."*

Why It Works: Straightforward, no drama, and it shows you're adaptable and ready for what's next.

The Need for a New Challenge - If you're after something fresh, say: *"I really enjoyed my time at [previous company], but after [number] years, I felt it was time for a new challenge. I'm looking for a role where I can take on bigger projects and bring fresh ideas to the table, which is why this opportunity caught my eye."*

Why It Works: You're positioning yourself as someone who's always looking to level up. It also subtly flatters the new company, since you're making it clear they're offering what you're seeking.

What *Not* to Say

- Don't say "I couldn't stand my boss," even if they were the human equivalent of a traffic jam. That's a major red flag.

- Don't bring up money as the #1 reason, unless you're applying for a role as a professional poker player. Keep it classy!

- "I just felt like it." That'll make you look like you're as focused as a squirrel on espresso.

- "I was bored and didn't have enough to do." Instead, talk about how you're looking for a new challenge, not just an excuse to nap under your desk.

- "I didn't get along with my coworkers." Reframe that with something like, "I'm looking for a role with a more collaborative, team-oriented vibe." No need to air office drama.

- "I was always working late, and it was affecting my personal life." Frame it as wanting a better work-life balance, not as a plea for someone to save you from your overloaded email inbox.

- "The company was going through layoffs." Instead, focus on how you're after a role with more stability—not a game of corporate musical chairs.

- "I felt undervalued." Say you're looking for a position where you can actually make an impact. Your future self will thank you.

- "I wanted a job that was easier." Talk about seeking a position that aligns with your skills and ambitions, not just one where you can coast through like it's a nap on a hammock.

- "I just need a job, any job." That's desperation, not ambition. Show them you've actually thought about the role and why it fits your goals.

- "I don't know anything about your company, but I'm sure it's great!" Do your homework! This isn't a blind date—you can't just show up and hope for the best.

- "I've never done that, but I'm sure I could figure it out." Great, but you're applying for the job, not the role of "experimental guinea pig." Confidence is key, but so is being realistic about your abilities.

- "I don't have any questions. I think you covered everything." It makes you look lazy. Always have at least one thoughtful question that shows you're engaged.

Chapter 7
Smart Questions to Ask—And the Ones You Should Skip

Here's the deal: preparing thoughtful questions for your interviewer isn't just a nice-to-have—it's absolutely essential! Believe it or not, about 90% of interviewers will wrap up the conversation by asking if you have any questions for them, yet only around 10% of candidates come prepared with solid inquiries. Don't be one of those caught off guard! This is your moment to shine, demonstrating that you've done your homework and that you're genuinely interested in the role.

Alright, my friend, it's time to strut your stuff with some intelligent questions for the interview! Think of this as your chance to dazzle—not just as a job seeker but as a curious superstar eager to dive into the company culture.

As you prepare your thoughtful questions, remember that the research you conducted about the company in Chapter 5 will be your secret weapon. Use that knowledge to craft insightful inquiries that showcase your genuine interest and understanding of the organization!

For instance, if you've done a little sleuthing (in the least creepy way possible) and discovered that the company is focused on transforming its digital services, you might ask, *"I noticed you're really leaning into those digital services. How does the team collaborate across departments to ensure these initiatives are a smashing success?"* This question not only shows that you're engaged but also highlights your awareness of the company's direction.

If you found out that the company is entering a new market, consider asking something like: *"I saw that your company recently expanded into the X market. How has that impacted your team's focus and strategy?"* This shows you're not just in it for the paycheck; you're genuinely invested in the company's growth and future.

Depending on the role you're applying for, here are more smart questions that could really make you shine (and might just earn you a gold star):

- ***"Can you tell me about the team I'd be working with?"*** It's a great way to learn about the people you'll spend most of your waking hours with and to see if you'd vibe with the team culture.

- ***"How would you describe your management style?"*** This helps you figure out if the leadership aligns with how you work best.

- ***"What does success look like in this role?"*** This shows you're not just here to collect a paycheck; you want to understand what makes the boss do a happy dance!

- ***"How does this team contribute to the overall goals of the company?"*** This demonstrates your interest in teamwork—because who wants to be the lone wolf in a den full of happy puppies?

- ***"What qualities do you think are most important for someone to thrive in this role?"*** This shows that you want to win and you don't mind start practicing!"

- ***"What is the biggest opportunity for improvement in this department right now?"*** You'll demonstrate problem-solving ambition and show that you're ready to roll up your sleeves.

- ***"What opportunities for professional development do the company offer?"*** This question signals that you're looking for a career, not just a pitstop on your way to the next snack break. Show them you're ready to level up!

- ***"Can you describe the company culture and the types of people who tend to succeed here?"*** This helps you figure out if you'd fit in better than a puzzle piece in a kid's playroom or if you'd be more like a square peg in a round hole. Plus, it shows you care about playing nicely with others!

- ***"What are the biggest challenges your company is gearing up for in the next five years?"*** Not only does this show you're forward-thinking, but it gives you a sneak peek into what you might be tackling if you get hired. Think of it as your chance to prepare for battle—no sword required!

- ***"Where do you see the organization in the next ten years?"*** This question lets you scope out the company's long-term vision and see if it aligns with your career goals. Who knows? You might even pick up some buzzwords to impress your friends later! It also indicates to your future employer that you're here for the long haul!

- ***"Are there opportunities for professional growth or continued learning within the company?"*** Asking this shows you're serious about developing your skills and staying with the company long-term.

- ***"How does the company support employees during challenging times?"*** This question digs into the company's values and how they treat their people during rough patches.

- ***"What excites you most about working here?"*** *This question highlights that you're looking for more than just a paycheck—you want a role that brings excitement and purpose to your work.*

- ***"Can you share why the previous Sales Manager left?"*** It's your chance to understand the company culture and get the inside scoop. However, tread carefully—make sure your interviewer is comfortable with straightforward questions. A well-timed question like this could earn you a nod of approval and but use your judgment to gauge the room!

- ***"What are the next steps in the hiring process?"*** This shows you're eager and ready to jump into action. Plus, you'll get a timeline to work with, so you can count down the days like a kid waiting for Christmas!

Now, let's talk about the don'ts. Avoid asking questions that scream, "I'm just here for the benefits!" For instance, steer clear of:

- "What are the employee benefits?" Seriously, you can find that out in the handbook later.

- "Can I leave early on Fridays?" You might as well ask for a permanent three-day weekend! Save that for once you're a rockstar employee—then you can maybe negotiate.

- "When can I expect my next pay rise?" It's way too early to be talking about money. Plus, they might not have the answer yet—and that's just awkward.

- "How many vacation days do I get?" Asking this can come off as a bit presumptuous. Let's focus on impressing them first—after all, you don't want them thinking you're just in it for the beach time!

- "How soon can I take a day off?" You haven't even started, and you're already planning your first escape? Not exactly inspiring confidence here.

- "Is it okay to work from home?" Asking this too early might imply you're already plotting your escape to the couch. Show them you're ready to roll up your sleeves first!

- "Will I have to work overtime?" Asking this too soon makes it sound like you're already dreading the workload. Let them know you're ready to bring your A-game—during regular hours.

- "What are the snacks in the pantry?" While we all appreciate free snacks, this is not the time to be wondering about the chip selection. Stay classy!

- "What's the turnover rate like?" This could raise red flags about your perception of the company culture. You're not auditioning for a horror movie, so keep the creepy questions at bay!

- "Can I get a raise after my first month?" This one screams impatience. It's like asking for dessert before finishing your meal—slow down and savor the experience!

- "Do you monitor internet usage?" Uh-oh. What are you planning to do online that's got you worried? Stay away from questions that raise eyebrows (or suspicion).

Chapter 8
Dressed to Kill or to Be Killed?

Congratulations! You've sent your CV, maybe hit refresh on your email a few times, and now you're just waiting to hear back. But here's the thing—when that interview invite does come, you don't want to be caught off guard. There's a whole lot more to prep than just knowing your own name and hoping you don't spill coffee on yourself. So, here's a checklist to make sure you're not just ready—you're *ready*.

Clothes: Because Sweatpants Won't Cut It

First things first—let's talk outfits. Look, I get it, your favorite pair of joggers might be calling your name, but this is not the time to answer. For interviews, think "polished but comfortable." You're not strutting the runway, but you also don't want to look like you've just rolled out of bed. A good rule of thumb: If you'd wear it to a wedding (but not as the bride or groom), you're probably safe.

Pro Tip #1: Before you even dig through your closet, go to the company's website or social media. Check out their team photos.

Applying to a tech startup
You'll probably be safe with a smart-casual vibe—think a crisp button-down or a sleek blouse paired with chinos, dark jeans, or a midi skirt. Bonus points for comfy-yet-polished shoes. You're

aiming for "I'm ready to brainstorm the next big thing," not "I just rolled out of bed."

Interviewing at a law firm or a bank
This is not the time to experiment with trends. Go for a tailored suit, a classic dress with understated accessories, or anything that screams "I can close deals and read the fine print." Even on their "casual Fridays," business formal usually reigns supreme.

Applying for a creative agency role
Here's where you can get a little playful. Think smart-casual but with a pop of personality—a colorful blazer, a quirky tie, or statement jewelry can show off your creativity. Just don't go overboard—you're still here to work, not host an art gallery opening.

Pro Tip #2: If you're really unsure, check out similar job postings in the same industry. You're applying to a marketing position at a creative agency? Look at what marketers are wearing in other companies' team photos. If everyone looks like they've just left a stylish coffee shop, that's your cue to aim for trendy-professional. But if they're rocking suits, maybe lean toward the more traditional side.

Industry Examples:
- **Tech Industry**: A software company might appreciate a laid-back look—think smart casual. Pair a nice blazer with jeans, or wear a simple dress with a statement necklace. You want to look approachable, but not too relaxed.

- **Finance/Corporate**: Here, you'll want to stick to business formal. A fitted suit, polished shoes, and maybe a tie for good measure. Yes, it's more buttoned-up (literally), but you don't want to look out of place in an environment where professionalism is key.

- **Creative/Marketing**: This is where you can show a little more personality in your attire. You can be slightly more playful with patterns or colors, as long as you're not looking like you're auditioning for a 90's sitcom. A sleek but quirky jacket or a sharp accessory can help you stand out—just not in neon.

Pro Tip #3: Try on the outfit the night before. Here's the deal—you don't want to wake up on interview day and discover your "go-to" blazer is now a "no-go." Maybe it shrank in the wash (or, let's be real, you grew into your love of snacks). Either way, scrambling to find an alternative at 7 a.m. is a surefire way to start your day with unnecessary stress and maybe even mismatched socks.

While you're at it, give your outfit the once-over. Check for stray threads, missing buttons, wrinkles, or—heaven forbid—that mysterious stain that's been lurking in plain sight. (How did I miss this? Is it coffee? Chocolate? Ink? The world may never know.)

Do a little "sit test." Can you sit down comfortably without the buttons threatening to pop off like confetti at a New Year's party? Can you bend over without flashing your life story to the room? Comfort and confidence go hand-in-hand—because nothing says "I'm nailing this interview" like pulling at a too-tight waistband mid-conversation.

Lastly, have a backup plan! Got pets or toddlers? Assume they'll spill, shed, or smudge your outfit right before you leave. Keep an emergency lint roller and a spare shirt or tie on standby. You'll thank yourself when chaos inevitably strikes.

The Dress Code Dilemma: Overdress or Underdress? Here's Why You Want to Avoid Both

Okay, so we've all heard the saying, "It's better to be overdressed than underdressed," but let's slow down for a minute. Sure, you definitely don't want to show up looking like you're headed to the beach (unless you're applying for a lifeguard gig), but going too fancy can also make things awkward. Let's break down the problems with both:

1. The Problem with Overdressing: You're Not at a Gala

Picture this: You walk into an interview for a marketing job at a cool tech startup, and everyone's rocking casual jeans and button-downs, while you're over there in a three-piece suit or a cocktail dress. Sure, you look like a million bucks, but the vibe? Awkward. It's like showing up to a backyard BBQ with a tray of hors d'oeuvres—impressive, but totally out of place.

Why It's a Problem: Overdressing can make it seem like you don't *quite* get the company culture. Employers want to know that you can blend into their team, and showing up in something way too formal might make them think you're out of touch or that you won't fit in with the laid-back vibe.

Example: You're applying for a graphic designer job and walk in wearing a formal suit, while everyone else is casually stylish. It might signal that you're overly corporate and maybe even a bit stiff—definitely not the free-spirited, creative energy they're hoping for.

2. The Problem with Underdressing: It's Not a Netflix Marathon

On the flip side, let's say you show up a little *too* casual. You're interviewing for a corporate role, but you roll in like it's Saturday brunch—t-shirt, jeans, and sneakers. Yikes. Now, not only do you look underprepared, but it also screams that you don't take the interview seriously. That's a big no-no.

Why It's a Problem: Underdressing shows a lack of effort and attention to detail, which isn't the first impression you want to make. Employers may wonder if that's how you'll approach your work, too—laid-back, but not in a good way. Plus, it's hard to feel confident when you know you're the most casually dressed person in the room.

Example: If you're going for a finance job and walk in with jeans and a casual shirt while everyone else is in sharp business attire, the hiring manager might immediately question your judgment. Even if you're qualified, this wardrobe blunder could overshadow your skills and experience.

3. Finding the Sweet Spot: The "Goldilocks" of Outfits

Not too formal, not too casual—your goal is to find that just right middle ground that says, "I belong here, but I'm also bringing my A-game." Think of it like being the Goldilocks of job interviews. You don't want to be overdressed and make the office manager in their sneakers feel awkward, nor do you want to underdress and have the hiring manager wondering if you got lost on your way to the farmer's market.

So, what's the solution? You want to find that "just right" middle ground. Here's a good rule: Dress one notch above what you think the day-to-day dress code is for the job. If it's a casual workplace, aim for smart-casual—think crisp jeans and a blazer. If the environment is business formal, break out that well-tailored suit. This shows that you respect the company's vibe while proving you've done your homework.

When it comes to your interview outfit, nail the "just right" look that respects the company's vibe while proving you've put thought into how you show up. Because first impressions matter, and nobody hires the person dressed like it's "laundry day."

Online Interview Look—No, You Can't Wear Your Pajamas!

When it comes to dressing for an online interview, all those principles for in-person interviews still apply—just remember, it's all about making a solid impression without looking like you just rolled out of bed.

Remember, even if your camera is only capturing the top half, dress as if you were going to meet the CEO for coffee. This means no pajama pants or fuzzy slippers! Picture this: you start nailing your answers, and then—bam!—the cat knocks something over, and you jump up to grab it, revealing your SpongeBob pajama bottoms. Not exactly the professional vibe you want to convey, right? Dressing fully gives you that extra boost of confidence, and you never know when you might need to do an impromptu dance to celebrate a great answer!

Online interviews can be tricky, and your background matters as much as your clothes! If your living space looks like a tornado hit it, hiring managers might wonder if you can handle a chaotic project. So, tidy up a bit—this isn't just for aesthetics; it's for your sanity, too!

A clean background helps you stay focused and shows you care about the little things. If you're unsure, just remember: the more neutral the backdrop, the less likely your grandma's "cat on a skateboard" painting will steal the show. And don't forget about lighting! Make sure your face is well-lit so you don't end up looking like a mysterious figure from a horror movie.

Chapter 9
The Big Interview Day – Mastering the Countdown

So, you've landed an interview—great job! Now, what's next? Plopping yourself in a chair and staring at the wall? Nope! Here's how to make the most of your time before the big day!

A.   Plan the Logistics

1. For In-person Meet-ups

On the day of the interview, your brain will already be juggling a million things, so let's eliminate the stress of running late or realizing you forgot your lucky socks. Here's how to set yourself up for a smooth and breezy experience:

Identify the Interview Location and Format—confirm the exact address, floor, and room—don't just wander into the break room thinking you're about to ace your interview!

Arrange Transportation. Traffic can be a sneaky beast—accidents, road closures, or that one guy who thinks it's a good idea to stop in the middle of the road to check his phone. To keep your cool, map out your route the night before and plan to leave early enough to account for all the unexpected delays. Aim to arrive 15-30 minutes ahead of time (and if you get there too early, grab a coffee and do some last-minute pep talks in the mirror). Trust me, it's way better than the panic of rolling in late!

Prepare Necessary Documents. Gather all your essential documents—resume, cover letter, references, and work portfolio—like you're assembling a superhero toolkit. Make several copies of each and stash them in a snazzy folder that says, "I'm professional and ready for action!"

2. For Online Interviews

Most importantly, remember to double-check the time and date— don't forget about that pesky time zone difference! Also, get the interviewer's telephone number as a backup contact in case something goes horribly wrong.

Start by checking your equipment. Ensure your computer or device is in good working order, with the necessary software downloaded and updated. If you're using an app like Zoom or Microsoft Teams, test it out in advance to make sure everything runs smoothly. There's nothing worse than logging in only to find you're stuck in a digital waiting room because you forgot to install the app!

Next, give your camera and microphone a quick check. Test the video and audio quality to ensure you're coming through loud and clear. No one wants to sound like they're broadcasting from a tin can or appear as if they're auditioning for a horror movie! And don't forget to ensure your phone or laptop is fully charged— there's nothing more awkward than having your device die mid-interview. If you're using a phone, keep your charger handy, just in case!

Also, have all your digital copies ready to go so you can share them with a click—no scrambling like you're on a game show when they ask for your portfolio!

Lastly, find a quiet, well-lit space for the interview. Natural light is your friend, but make sure it doesn't create a glare on your screen. Clear away any potential distractions, like your pet's latest toy collection or the laundry basket that's become a fixture in your background. A tidy, distraction-free environment helps you stay focused and shows your commitment to making a great impression!

B. Upon Arrival at the Interview Location

1. Say Hi to the Gatekeepers (aka Receptionists)

When arrive, don't just breeze past the receptionists like a stealthy ninja! Instead, greet the receptionist with a friendly "hello." These folks control public opinion in the office, and trust me, a little politeness can go a long way. Think of them as the all-seeing oracle of the workplace—they know who brings the doughnuts and who's just there for the coffee. They might mention your "great smile" to the boss, or they could just as easily say, "That one? They looked like they were auditioning for a horror movie." If you get hired, you'll have a well-informed friend who can share insider gossip and the best lunch spots. So, don't underestimate the power of a warm greeting!

2. Channel Your Inner Spy

While you wait, take a good look around. Is the office buzzing with energy, or is it as quiet as a library during finals week? If there are any company magazines or materials lying around, grab them! They might provide some last-minute intel on the company that could come in handy. Also, pay attention to the employees: Do they look like they enjoy their lives, or are they on the verge of a coffee-fueled meltdown? Observing the vibe can give you talking points for the interview and help you gauge if this is the kind of place you'd want to work—or if you should make a mental note to run in the opposite direction.

3. Review Your Game Plan

Pretend you're Tom Brady reviewing plays. Whip out those interview notes and give them one last look. It's like cramming for a test, but cooler. Focus on a few key points you want to hit—like why you're amazing—and any clever questions you've got lined up. Don't try to memorize everything; that'll just make you more nervous. Instead, aim to remember a handful of essential points that highlight your skills and fit for the role. This way, when the interviewer throws a question your way, you'll feel more at ease and confident. You'll thank yourself later when your brain doesn't freeze up mid-question!

4. Rehearse Your Intro Like It's a Broadway Audition

Quick, what's your name and why do you want this job? Got your elevator pitch? Run through it in your head (or, if you're feeling bold, out loud under your breath). When they call your name, you want to drop that polished intro like a pro—no stammering or fumbling around like you just forgot your lines on stage! Imagine walking in and delivering your pitch with the confidence of a Broadway performer. Remember, this is your moment to impress, so make it unforgettable!

5. Don't Let Nerves Win

If your heart's pounding like you just ran a marathon, take a sec to breathe. Yeah, I know—easier said than done! But a few deep breaths can work wonders. If possible, take a short walk or stretch before your interview. Think of it as your pre-game warm-up! Light physical activity can help release pent-up energy and calm your nerves. Plus, strutting around like you're on a catwalk might just help you channel your inner superstar. And don't forget, dehydration can exacerbate feelings of anxiety, so keep yourself hydrated to stay focused. At the end of the day, don't worry; everyone in that building has been in your shoes before!

6. Quick Mirror Check

Don't get caught fixing your hair in the middle of the lobby—unless you want to give everyone a show. Instead, sneak away for a bathroom break to ensure you're looking sharp and free of any embarrassing surprises, like spinach in your teeth right before shaking hands with your future boss. While you're in there, do a quick once-over: check your hair, make sure your shirt isn't inside out, and confirm your deodorant is still doing its job. You want to walk into that interview exuding confidence, not the lingering scent of panic. So, freshen up and come out ready to dazzle!

7. Where to Sit Determines whether you'll Get a Seat

If you find yourself in a waiting room, resist the urge to slump in your chair like you've just run a marathon. You want to look engaged, not like you're prepping for a job as a statue. A good posture sends a message that you're confident and ready to take on the challenge.

When it's finally your turn to enter the interview room, remember this golden rule: don't just plop down in the first chair you see like you're claiming the best seat at a concert! Wait for the interviewer to guide you to the right spot. Think of it like a fancy dinner party—wait for the host to show you to your seat. If nobody comes to lead you, use your common sense and avoid getting trapped in any weird situations.

And then there's the interviewee who boldly takes the chairman's seat at the head of the table. While confidence is great, this move can make you come off as presumptuous, giving the impression that you see yourself as the boss rather than a job seeker. It's a classic case of misreading the room! So, remember, your seating choice matters, be mindful of where you sit. This small gesture can set the tone for a successful and smooth interview!

Once you sit down, take a moment to adjust your seat for comfort and visibility—just like when you first sit in a car. Make sure you're at an angle that allows you to make eye contact with the interviewer—because nobody wants to be that person craning their neck like a giraffe trying to spot a snack. A little adjustment can go a long way in ensuring you feel relaxed and ready to shine!

Here's one of my personal pet peeves as an interviewer: Imagine this—I walk into the room, and the interviewee plops down on the chair right next to the door. Sounds harmless, right? Except now, I can't even open the door properly without an awkward shuffle or risk smacking them with it!

It's not just about logistics—it's about awareness. The lack of thoughtfulness in such a simple decision sets the tone for the entire interview. It makes me wonder: If they can't consider where

I might sit in this small room, how will they handle bigger responsibilities that require attention to detail and consideration for others? First impressions matter, and let me tell you, making me struggle to get to my own chair is not a good one.

8. Mastering the Art of the First Impression

When the interviewer walks in, it's time to snap out of your daydream and shift into interview mode. Why? Because research shows most interviewers form an opinion in the first five seconds—that's right, they're sizing you up before you've even sat down. First impressions matter, so here's how to make those fleeting moments work in your favor.

Stand up confidently as they approach, maintaining a calm and composed demeanor. Flash a warm, genuine smile that says, "I'm excited to be here!" Then, it's time for the handshake. Aim for a firm grip that feels confident—not bone-crushing (you're here to land the job, not send your interviewer to A&E). A limp handshake is just as bad, leaving them wondering if you left your confidence at home.

And don't forget the eye contact! A steady gaze of about 2–3 seconds is perfect. It shows you're engaged and self-assured without veering into awkward staring territory. Any longer, and you might feel like you're auditioning for a romance drama. Remember, this is an interview, not Love at First Sight.

By combining a firm handshake, natural eye contact, and a friendly smile, you'll nail that critical first impression—even if your inner voice is yelling, "Run!"

9. Be a Good Listener and Spark the Right Vibe

When the interview starts, don't just focus on listing all the things you know and have done—make sure you're hearing them too. Being a good listener is key to building a connection. Nod, maintain eye contact, and show genuine interest in what they're saying. Think of it like a ping-pong match: let their words guide your responses and create a natural flow. This way, you'll come across as a real, engaging human rather than a lifeless cyborg. And trust me, this human touch is what will set you apart from all the other cyborgs in the running!

Pay attention to the interviewer's tone and pace, and match it subtly—it's like mirroring, and trust me, it'll get you far! Remember, interviews are as much about chemistry as they are about qualifications. They aren't hiring your CV; they're hiring you! So, let your personality shine and aim to win the heart of the interviewer before you leave the room. I once had an interviewer—who later became my CEO—tell me, 'You charmed me to death!' And no, it wasn't my dazzling good looks that did the trick (though it might have helped!). It was the genuine connection I built during our conversation. People want to work with someone they feel a spark with, so show them why you're the one they can't resist bringing on board.

C. The All-Important Follow-Up

So, the interview is done? Awesome! But hold your horses—there's one last step: the follow-up email. Keep it short and sweet—thank them for their time and throw in a specific detail from the interview that resonated with you. Nobody wants to read a novel here; it's just a friendly nudge to say, "Hey, I'm still here, and I'm still interested!"

Not sure what to say? Try these:

"Thanks for the insightful conversation today! I'm really pumped about the possibility of becoming a valued member of [Company Name] and bringing my experience in consultative selling to the team. Looking forward to the next steps!"

"Thanks for taking the time to meet with me today! I really enjoyed learning about the mission of your company, which resonates perfectly with mine. I'm genuinely excited about the opportunity to contribute!"

"It was a pleasure meeting with you today. I loved hearing about [specific project] and can't wait to bring my skills to your team. If you need any further info, just let me know!"

D.   Keep the recruitment Agent in the Loop

After an interview, if you landed the opportunity through a recruitment agent, it's essential to give them a call—not just as a courtesy, but as a smart strategic move. Think of your recruitment agent as your behind-the-scenes cheerleader. They're not just the ones who got you through the door; they can also play a pivotal role in what happens next.

A quick thank-you call does more than show gratitude—it keeps you fresh in their mind. If they have a good impression of you, they're more likely to advocate for you when the employer asks for feedback. Agents often provide insights to hiring managers that go beyond what's on your CV, and a glowing endorsement can tip the scales in your favor.

But what if you don't get short-listed this time? That's where keeping your agent in the loop really pays off. A professional relationship with them means you're at the top of their list when similar roles come up. They'll remember your enthusiasm, your skills, and the fact that you treated them with respect—qualities that make you their go-to candidate for future opportunities.

I remember this happening to me—I wasn't short-listed for one job, but because I stayed in touch and thanked the agent, they called me the very next day with a second opportunity. That new interview led to a job offer, and as it turns out, I absolutely love the role!

Recruitment agents aren't just intermediaries; they're your allies in the job market. Keeping them informed and appreciated ensures they'll continue to support you—whether it's advocating for you now or connecting you to the next big opportunity. So, pick up the phone and make that call. It's a small gesture with big potential benefits.

Chapter 10
Post-interview – Time to Relax (But Don't Get Too Cozy!)

So, you made it through the interview without spilling coffee on your shirt or accidentally calling your interviewer "Mom." That alone is a win. But if you think your work here is done, I'm going to stop you right there! Nope. There's a whole post-interview strategy that can make you stand out even more. So kick off your shoes, but keep your thinking cap on. Here's how to become that unforgettable candidate they just *have* to hire.

1. The Thank-You Note – A Little Politeness with a Big Purpose

Yes, your mom was right about writing thank-you notes, but this one is not just polite; it's part of your grand job-winning strategy. And guess what? A quick, generic "Thanks for your time!" just won't cut it. You want this thank-you to be like the encore at a concert – leave them wanting more.

Example:
"Dear [Interviewer's First Name] – I loved discussing the [Job Title] role with you and was thrilled to hear more about your exciting plans for [project or initiative they mentioned]. Thanks for sharing your vision! And I hope the expansion doesn't involve more battles with that finicky coffee machine – I completely sympathize! Looking forward to possibly joining the team and taking the caffeine challenge alongside you all."

Throw in a funny callback to something from the interview – the malfunctioning coffee machine, the office dog that barked mid-question, or how you both can't remember the last time you actually understood a full conversation over Zoom – just something that reminds them of the rapport you built in the room.

2. Beef Up Your Follow-Up: The Interview Leftovers

Remember that moment in the interview when they asked if you had experience in "strategic widget optimization" or something equally vague, and you said, "Oh, sure!" – but afterward, you realized you totally forgot to explain how you actually *rock* at that? Here's your chance to shine!

Example:
"You know, I've been thinking about our chat regarding 'strategic widget optimization' and realized I left out a recent example. At my last job, I helped streamline widget delivery times by 20% by implementing a new tracking tool and setting up weekly check-ins with the team. Happy to dive deeper into this if it's helpful!"

Boom. Now they see you as thoughtful and proactive, not the person who zoned out when they started talking widgets. Adding examples and ideas they didn't hear the first time gives you another chance to sell yourself.

3. Bring Out the Big Guns: The 30-60-90 Day Plan (How to Really Impress Them)

Drafting a 30-60-90 day plan isn't just for type-A go-getters; it's for anyone who wants to *land* that job. Yes, it might sound intense, but it's your way of saying, "Here's what I'll do to make your lives easier, starting Day 1."

But keep it simple. You don't need to map out a 100-page manifesto. Just outline a few clear, action-packed steps and toss in a bit of personality. Make them feel you're already part of the team and know how to take the wheel.

Example Outline:
30 Days – The "Getting to Know Me" Phase
- *Meet the Team & Product: Learn what the company does, how it does it, and who I'll be working with. Get cozy with the product (and don't be shy to ask questions).*
- *Market Research: Time to stalk the competition and know what makes our product the hero of the industry.*
- *CRM Familiarization: Get friendly with the sales tools. It's like my new digital assistants.*
- *Start Calling: Make those first calls to prospects. It's okay if I'm a little nervous – everyone's been there!*

60 Days – Getting My Groove On
- *Perfect My Pitch: Adjust my spiel, work on my charm, and start handling objections like a pro.*
- *Own My Pipeline: Manage my own list of prospects and leads. Time to juggle, but in a super organized way.*
- *Customer Connections: Deepen relationships with potential clients. They're not just leads; they're future customers.*
- *Ask for Feedback: Check in with my manager. I'm not perfect (yet), but I'm improving every day.*

90 Days – The Sales Rockstar Phase
- *Hit Those Targets: By now, it's time to start meeting (or smashing) my sales goals. I got this!*
- *Sell More to Existing Clients: Look for those golden upsell opportunities. I'm the gift that keeps on giving.*
- *Refine My Strategy: Fine-tune my sales tactics. What's working? Double down on it.*
- *Collaborate Like a Boss: Keep syncing with other teams to keep clients happy and sales flowing.*
- *Celebrate My Wins: Reflect on what I've learned and set new goals. I'm officially a sales superstar.*

With something like this, they can picture you doing the job, making their life easier, and even saving the team from daily coffee machine meltdowns. Now they know you're a problem-solver who takes initiative and has a sense of humor.

4. Find Them on LinkedIn (in a Non-Stalker Way)

The post-interview LinkedIn add is delicate. First, no weird messages like, "Hey, remember me???" Keep it light. Send a request with a note along the lines of, "Thanks again for the great conversation! Loved hearing about [specific thing]. Would be great to stay connected."

When they accept, hit the brakes. No over-liking or nonstop commenting on their posts about supply chain innovations or dog-sitting tips. Just a simple message will do. LinkedIn presence is great; LinkedIn shadowing is not.

Example:
"Hi [Interviewer's First Name], I really enjoyed meeting you and learning more about the team at [Company Name]. Looking forward to staying connected!"

Now they can keep you on their radar without feeling like they're being cyberstalked by a candidate from a true-crime documentary.

5. Be Patient – It's the Home Stretch

After all these strategic moves, now comes the hardest part: waiting. Resist the urge to follow up every day. Remind yourself they have a process, and constant follow-ups won't speed it up. But don't totally go silent either! If you haven't heard anything a week after your thank-you note, feel free to send a casual, short check-in.

Example:
"Hi [Interviewer's First Name], I just wanted to follow up and see if there's been any update regarding the [Job Title] role. I'm still very interested and excited about the opportunity and would love to contribute to [mention project or goal you discussed]."

Remember, your goal is to seem eager – not desperate. This is like dating: play it cool but let them know you're still interested!

Wrapping It All Up

These steps might sound small, but together they create an impression that's hard to forget. You're organized, thoughtful, proactive – and hey, a little funny too. By going above and beyond with a thank-you, sharing additional insights, and sketching out a mini-plan, you'll show them that hiring you isn't just a good choice; it's the *only* choice. Now, go on, hit send on that thank-you note, and picture yourself nailing your first day on the job!

1. Follow-up Email for Business Development Manager Position

Subject: Thank You for the Opportunity

Dear [Hiring Manager's Name],

I wanted to extend my sincere thanks for the opportunity to interview for the Business Development Manager role at [Company's Name]. It was a pleasure speaking with you and learning more about the company's ambitious growth goals and commitment to delivering innovative solutions in [industry/field].

The insights you shared about [specific topic discussed, e.g., upcoming projects or challenges] were particularly exciting, and I am eager to bring my experience in strategic growth and relationship-building to contribute to these initiatives. I am confident that my background in developing and executing impactful sales strategies aligns well with [Company's Name]'s objectives.

Thank you once again for the opportunity. Please do not hesitate to reach out if I can provide any additional information to assist with your decision-making process. I look forward to the possibility of working together to drive [Company's Name] toward even greater success.

Warm regards,

[Your Full Name]

2. Follow-up Email for Administrative Assistant Position

Subject: Thank You for the Interview

Dear [Hiring Manager's Name],

Thank you for the opportunity to interview for the Administrative Assistant role at [Company's Name]. I enjoyed our conversation and am even more enthusiastic about the chance to join your team and support your operations in such a dynamic environment.

Hearing about [specific detail discussed in the interview, e.g., upcoming office changes or tools being implemented] helped me envision how I could bring my organizational skills and customer service experience to streamline processes and improve efficiency. I am particularly excited about [mention any aspect of the role that resonated with you, e.g., a specific project or responsibility], and I am confident that my proactive approach will allow me to make a positive contribution.

Thank you once again for the wonderful opportunity. I look forward to the possibility of working together, and please feel free to reach out if there's anything further, I can provide to assist with your decision.

Best regards,

[Your Full Name]

3. Follow-up Email for Internship Position

Subject: Thank You for the Opportunity

Dear [Hiring Manager's Name],

I wanted to reach out and thank you for the opportunity to interview for the internship at [Company's Name]. It was fantastic to learn more about the team and the innovative projects underway. I am very excited about the potential to contribute and grow within such a respected organization.

During our conversation, I was particularly inspired by [mention something specific discussed in the interview, like a project or skill you're eager to develop], and I am eager to apply my research and communication skills to support [Company's Name]'s objectives. I am confident that my enthusiasm and commitment will allow me to make a positive contribution during my time as an intern.

Thank you again for the opportunity, and please do not hesitate to contact me if you need any additional information. I look forward to the possibility of joining your team!

Sincerely,

[Your Full Name]

About the Author

With over 15 years of experience running a successful business consultancy, Christine Frey knows exactly what it takes to thrive in the professional world. She's held senior management roles at multinational corporations, managed teams of over 100 people, and personally recruited more than 1,000 employees, conducting thousands of interviews along the way. After all that, she's practically a recruiter mind reader.

But Christine's not just the one asking the tough questions—she's been on the other side of the table too. Her early career as an interviewee taught her what works, what doesn't, and how to stand out in a competitive job market.

Drawing from her deep experience on both sides of the hiring table, Christine shares what recruiters are really looking for, the biggest mistakes job seekers make (hint: it's not just typos), and how to fix them. She also reveals secret tips that nobody ever tells you—strategies that will give you the edge and make you unforgettable. Whether you're crafting a standout CV or preparing to crush your next interview, Christine provides actionable tips and insider secrets to help you land your dream job—without breaking a sweat or losing your sense of humor along the way.

"Step-by-Step Guide" Series

Step-by-Step Guide is your ultimate toolkit for mastering life's most important challenges with clarity, confidence, and a dose of humor. Whether you're navigating your career, building stronger relationships, raising happy kids, managing your money, or dreaming of launching your own business, this series is packed with everything you need to reach your goals. Forget vague advice and abstract theories—*Step-by-Step Guide* gives you proven strategies and actionable, practical guidance tailored to real-life scenarios, showing you exactly how to turn your boldest goals into manageable milestones.

Each book in the *Step-by-Step Guide* series is written by a seasoned expert who doesn't just talk the talk—they've walked the walk. These authors bring years of hands-on experience, deep knowledge, and hard-earned success in their fields to every page. You're learning from someone who's been there, done that, and is now sharing the secrets of their success. Full of real-world insights and little-known tips, these books are as authentic as they are actionable.

Ready to turn your dreams into action? Your next chapter begins here!

Also, look out for our upcoming titles:
- *The Ultimate workplace survival kit: Mastering the Office Jungle*
- *Next-Level Career Moves: Unlock Your Potential*
- *The Personal Brand Blueprint: Stand Out and Succeed*

Next Chapter Press

www.ingramcontent.com/pod-product-compliance
Lightning Source LLC
Chambersburg PA
CBHW040759150426
42811CB00056B/1074